BEAGLE TALES 9

BY

BOB FORD

SUNBURY
P R E S S ®

Mechanicsburg, PA USA

Published by Sunbury Press, Inc.
Mechanicsburg, PA USA

SUNBURY
P R E S S ®
www.sunburypress.com

FIRST SUNBURY PRESS EDITION: July 2024

Set in Adobe Garamond Pro | Interior design by Crystal Devine | Cover by Lawrence Knorr | Edited by Lawrence Knorr.

Publisher's Cataloging-in-Publication Data
Names: Ford, Bob, author.
Title: Beagle tales 9 / Bob Ford.
Description: First trade paperback edition. | Mechanicsburg, PA : Sunbury Press, 2024.
Summary: In Ford's ninth collection of outdoor humor he continues to strike a chord with hunters and dog lovers as he makes observations about contemporary life, often through nostalgic narratives of the simpler days of his youth (way back in the 1900s).
Identifiers: ISBN : 979-8-88819-228-3 (paperback).
Subjects: PETS / Dogs / Breeds | SPORTS & RECREATION / Hunting | HUMOR / Topic / Animals.

Designed in the USA
0 1 1 2 3 5 8 13 21 34 55

For the Love of Books!

SOLSTICE SOLITUDE

When the rush of the holidays has passed and the winter solstice has passed, that is when you can find me seeking the solitude of the pines. Don't get me wrong, I am a devoted houndsman, and I run beagles year-round. Moreover, I love those early autumnal hunts, as the dogs bust into the goldenrod and crop fields in dogged pursuit after the rabbits. I love an hour-long chase in a cornfield as the rabbit runs his maze in the maize, attempting to elude the dogs. I wait patiently by the edge of the cornfield, knowing that eventually, the rabbit will bust out of the corn and head back to the goldenrod where the chase started—back where the groundhog holes are plentiful and escape is promised. Winter hunting, where I live, is a different matter. The frost and snow have killed the goldenrod, the corn has been harvested, and the rabbits will have moved on to places where there is more cover to protect them from weasels, fox, coyote, fisher, hawks, owls, mink—everything that eats meat will kill bunnies. Rabbits run in their various circles, all typically intersecting close to the spot where the chase starts, and the ensuing music from the hounds is something that I pursue even when the weather seems too uncomfortable for many to go outside.

There are thick patches of multi-floral rose and greenbrier that I hunt in the winter, but I really enjoy finding a stand of pines or hemlocks. Here in Pennsylvania, there is a lot of public land, and much of it is reclaimed surface mines purchased by the state after the coal was removed. Pine trees have shallow roots, and therefore, they are well suited to growing in a place where much of the topsoil has been removed. As the grasses and weeds succumb to the dropping temperatures and shortened days, the rabbits will concentrate into the conifers, and that is where the hound song erupts.

January and February are blissful months in the field. We are past the bustle of the archery rut. The woods aren't full like they are in the rifle season for deer. The stocked pheasants that attract people from far and wide have all been harvestedor are very low in number. In other words, you can get some real solitude in those late winter hunts. The winter solstice marks the beginning of my time for renewal and hound work that can shine at a time of year when many beagles struggle.

You often hear beaglers talk about a "snow dog" and all that it can offer. Scenting is poor on the snow compared to a dew-drenched October morning. More than that, as a rabbit disturbs the snow and it melts a little, it will happen that the tracks that are left first (older) will have snow that melts more than the most recently run tracks. That, of course, is logical, but on certain days, the increased moisture will hold more scent, and this can result in the scent getting weaker as the dogs get closer to the rabbit. In other words, the scent smells better if the pack were to go backward, and we all know that backtracking is one of the worst words in any hound hunter's vocabulary—a veritable cuss word and vulgarity that no one wants to hear! It is one of the worst things you can say about a dog and an insult that you don't haul out of your pocket to hurl at your friend's beloved pooch without good reason.

"Your dog is backtracking!" That is a sentence that has caused some conflict. I love to watch beagles run in the snow, and I love to watch all the hard work of year-round training and conditioning pay off with the snow, causing no big problems. A really rabbit-wise beagle will learn to utilize their eyes to see the tracks that the rabbit leaves in the snow on days with fresh powder or a snowpack where the surface is soft enough to allow the light rabbit to leave tracks. You would think that all beagles would learn to do this, but they are so driven by their noses that this use of the visual

2

to augment the olfactory data never happens frequently enough for anyone's kennel of rabbit runners. I have a few that look for tracks. My old Duke dog was with me in Cape Cod, hunting on the beach on November day. At one point, the rabbit left all the cover and ran along the beach. The only dog barking on the scent was Duke, and he was looking for the tiny tracks left in wet sand! By comparison, a rabbit track left in the snow is massive. Very often, when there has been a break in the baying music of the hounds, and the rabbit has managed to trick the dogs, it will happen that the silence is broken by the voice of a hound that I know is prone to using the eyes to assist in the chase.

In the slalom of pines, I can see a lot of the chase, the brown cottontail scampering through the evergreens. Often, you can see the rabbit when it is way too far to shoot. That is not a problem for me, as the chorus of dogs—with their various voices merged—rings through the trees and nurtures my being. One hound's chop, chop, chop mixed with another's rolling bawl, and all of that added to a higher-pitched squall from a third hound. I like just to remain motionless and wait for a closer shot and just soak in the music, a song that stirs my soul and warms my body as I brace my back to the winter wind. I will seek the solace of the pines for a little while each day in the winter, and my goal is always to get a great chase. I rarely shoot more than one rabbit.

Sometimes, when the crusted snow thaws and freezes again, and no powder falls for days or weeks—those arctic high-pressure days when the sky is sunny and blue as frigid air pours down to the ground—the resulting conditions leave the ground akin to peanut brittle. No melting snow. No good scent. On those days I find that I will seldom take a quartet or even a trio to sing me the song of the chase, but rather a duo or a solo. Beagles will tend to get competitive for rabbit scent, and when said scent is so faint the combined zeal of the dogs can make the pack really struggle. Last year had many days like that in February. Plenty of rabbit hunters were getting few chases or none. Others were getting chases that rapidly ended before the dogs could circle the rabbit. I was getting a few rabbits with my smallest beagle, Diamond, Duke's daughter. It was tough to get a shot because the crunchy crust made it almost impossible to relocate. The rabbit has two big ears that are always tuned into noises that might represent a threat. As a result, I ended up standing wherever I was when the chase started. Typically, I will move to a spot where a better shot might be possible—an intersection of two paths in the pines or a small opening inside a ring of trees. The loud snow forced me to be a statue.

It would take a long time for the rabbit to forget about me and return since I could not relocate with any success. Meanwhile, Diamond just kept pursuing the rabbit, her voice more like a scream—an "AAAAAAH" that emerges from her tiny body. She is ten inches tall at the shoulder and only fourteen pounds in weight. She can disappear in deep, powdery snow, but she is small enough that she very often stays on the surface of a crusted snow when my heavier hounds will break through the snow and sink to their bellies. The rabbits in front of Diamond must have wondered how she could stay so relentless, seemingly floating on the snow. Her voice was like a banshee as the rabbit made loops through the pines. Every day, the two of us would go home, one rabbit in the vest and Diamond in the passenger seat of the cab. The thousand-dollar, insulated dog box that sat in the bed of the truck was unused, as I was only taking one dog—Diamond. My wife and I were making scotch eggs with ground rabbit meat, slow-cooking rabbit stew, and getting inventive with rabbit piccata and French onion soup made with stock made from rabbit bones.

The long, cold winter was sapping the joy from many of my friends, as they were outside solely to go to work, shovel the sidewalks, or go to the store. I would wake early and start work immediately so that I could be free for those last two hours of daylight, alone in the pines. There were houses less than a mile or two away, but if I got into the middle of the pines, I could almost pretend I was in the wilderness; no one was venturing afield to be where Diamond and I were hunting. We were finding ourselves not beleaguered by the winter but rather energized and renewed in that peaceful place. It felt like the movie *Groundhog Day*, except it was Rabbit Hunting Day. Another day when work was started early, completed, and we rushed into the pines for local protein. Unlike the movie, it was a joyful repetition. Each rabbit had a different strategy. Each chase had its idiosyncrasies. Some days, I didn't get a rabbit.

There was one rabbit that was always jumped near a tangle of red briar at the edge of the pines. I could never get a shot at it. It always holed or escaped. Often, Diamond would get another rabbit up and running after the red briar bunny defeated us. But I noticed that the red briar rabbit always went to the top of the hill at some point. There was a gap there were two different stands of pines almost met. It was like two peninsulas that almost met in the vastness of an ocean of open ground, void of cover. But it never went there until late in the chase, right before it would ghost us.

On Leap Day, the last day of the season, we jumped the red briar bunny, and I immediately walked the long way around a big field to silently reach that little opening between the two stands of pines, a sort of Strait of Gibraltar connecting two continents of conifers. I waited an hour; the song of the hunt was far off. Then the music got louder. The rabbit was coming. It was getting dark, and out came the red briar rabbit. It stopped, I think, startled to see me. I shouldered my Ugartechea side by side and slid the safety off in one motion; I pointed the proven rabbit gun at the rabbit, and the red-brier bunny stood there for five seconds. Then, I just let him go. He crossed from one stand of pines to the other as I opened the side-by-side shotgun and removed the shells. I put the removable leather sling on the shotgun and rested it on my shoulder. I caught Diamond when she emerged and said, "Tomorrow is March 1, the start of meteorological spring. This has been a wonderful winter, little girl. And I put her on my shoulders and carried her to the truck.

Getting Ready for Christmas

A big part of the weeks leading into Christmas in Pennsylvania is the two-week rifle season for deer. Now, I am a beagle guy. We hunt rabbits a lot, but there is no rabbit hunting permitted during the rifle season for deer. This causes extreme problems in my house, as I will leave early in the morning to hunt deer, and the dogs get confused that they do not get to go with me. Typically, when I leave the house in the wee hours of the morning, it is to rabbit hunt. The dogs get loaded into the dog box, and we leave together.

Furthermore, while I am personally biased and think my beagles are very intelligent, they still have not learned how to differentiate a rifle from a shotgun. They know I am going hunting, and to be honest, they lose their minds and erupt into a howling, bawling, boisterous cacophony that reaches decibel levels that will wake the dead. Oh, did I mention that the dogs live in the house? Or that my wife, Renee, is a light sleeper? Yeah, there is that. As I am driving to the hardwoods at five o'clock in the morning, Renee is dealing with a pack of hunting beagles pouncing on her and sounding the alarm that her husband has obviously developed dementia because he went hunting with no dogs. Zero. Zilch. Nada.

I mean, I have six dogs, and I often take just a couple of them, and that causes problems as they have to take turns, but when they all get left home, it is just a big ball of confusion. Renee likes to sleep until eight, then ease into a cup of coffee and then a second cup with a bagel or toast. By nine o'clock she is caffeinated so and civil and at work. Oh, waking up in the dark is not her preference and never will be. Then, there is the butchering process when a deer is brought home. You can't let dogs chase deer in Pennsylvania, so I have to go in through the garage and remove all my hunting clothes to be washed and purified of deer scent. I work too hard to get these dogs trained to let them think deer scent is allowable. Oh, then there is the butchering,

I am too cheap to pay a butcher to process my venison, so I do it myself. I also do not own a band saw, so I deboned the deer. The front legs generally become burger, and the hind legs get separated into the three large muscle groups. Those groups can then become roasts, cut into steaks, or sometimes turned into burger or stew meat. I usually get two doe tags, and butchering can be a sustained effort, depending on the amount of success in the field. When I get a buck and two does, it can be a few nights of butchering, and this means the mutts are all about the smell of raw meat in the kitchen. Hey, it is all part of the process, and the dogs get a little meat, too. I have never believed that the meat itself will induce them to be deer runners because I have never seen them chase cows, pigs, or even chickens. That being said, butchering meat adds that extra bit of chaos with the hunting house dogs. They might surf a table or counter after I am done.

So, due to all the extra stress, I like to be extra nice to Renee after deer season is over and all the meat is frozen. I started to sit with her and watch these Christmas movies that she likes on Hallmark Channel. They are all pretty similar, as I told Renee when I said, "These things are all alike!"

"What?"

"It is a cookie-cutter script."

"What do you mean?"

"Well," I said, "A wildly successful woman leaves the big city for Christmas and either goes back to her hometown in the middle of nowhere, or she breaks down in the middle of nowhere and has to spend Christmas there. Then what? She meets the best man who has ever lived, and somehow, he is neither married nor dating anyone! They hit it off, but there is a snag in the relationship, and they have this time of tension. Maybe she has an ex-boyfriend show up. Ultimately, the gal gets back with the small-town boy, and they get married. She moves her business from Manhattan to the picturesque rural hamlet. The dude usually owns a dog."

"Maybe they are a little similar," Renee said.

"And I know why you like them so much."

"Oh really?" she raised her eyebrows in disbelief.

"Yep," I said, "They remind you of how you met me, and now you are in the country too. All these movies are Christmas romance novels, and you like to remember about our life together."

Renee said, "Oh, I wish you came with just one dog!" she yelled as she struggled to extract her legs from the sleeping weight of six beagles so she could get up and get a mug of eggnog.

Weird Potluck

For as long as I can remember, Thanksgiving has been almost synonymous with rabbit hunting, as every Thanksgiving starts with a rabbit hunt. This practice goes back to my childhood when Dad and I would leave the house early and hunt all day to avoid the conflict that is intrinsically part of any situation where two women share the same kitchen, and this conflict is magnified when those two women are related. Very often, my grandmother would come to our house for Thanksgiving or a big part of the day, and she and her daughter (my Mom) could not get along when they were in the kitchen.

Keep in mind that this was back in the days when houses were not nearly as big as they are being built today. Our kitchen table was shoved against the wall, which allowed four people to sit comfortably. That was the standard configuration most of the time—Dad, Mom, my sister, and me. Now, we could pull the table away from the wall, allowing two more people to sit on that side, but this centered the table in the kitchen and made it almost impossible to move around the room. We could fit four more people if we not only pulled the table away from the wall but also inserted a leaf into the table, making it longer. Now, we could fit eight people. Flying in an airplane has more comfortable seating in comparison to my childhood dinner table at the holidays. The close-quarter nature of our kitchen only made the tensions worse between Mom and Gram, as they were constantly in each other's way.

One thing that is odd about me is that even though my job requires me to be rather extroverted at times, I am an introvert by nature, and I can easily be content with solitude. Well, I call it solitude; my wife, Renee, just tells me that I am antisocial. The COVID Thanksgiving last year was rather nice for me—it was just my wife and I! We ate the traditional fare at our place—wild game—and it was a relaxing day. In fact, the strict lockdowns in town had my wife so full of cabin fever that she actually went rabbit hunting with me on Thanksgiving morning,

"Hey, the dogs are chasing!" Renee yelled.

"Shh."

"What?"

"Well, now the rabbit knows where we are."

"So what?" Renee rolled her eyes.

"I will have to relocate to get a shot. Where is your shotgun?"

"I left it in the truck."

"Why?"

"You know I miss rabbits bad," she said, "And I think we have plenty in the freezer already."

"Okay, well, flank this ridge, and if the dogs get moving towards the hardtop road, catch them. I will move down to try and get a shot after it circles. Feel free to be as loud as you want up there so the rabbit doesn't try to go that way."

After our quarantined feast, Renee went to her mother's apartment, where she had supper with traditional fare—stuffing, turkey from the store, mashed potatoes, and all that stuff.

Just recently, Renee was bopping around the kitchen and humming as she was whipping up a batch of rabbit stew. "Looks good!" I said.

"Test run," she answered.

"For what?"

"Oh, nothing." She shifted around the room.

"No, you didn't?" I asked.

"I can't wait for this, so don't you spoil this for me; I am taking this recipe when we go next week. I can't wait for a non-quarantined holiday season!" I knew instantly what she was talking about. It was the odd meal we had a couple of years ago. Renee and her gal pals always love to get together and have these little-themed gatherings. Any excuse will do, and it can be a bumper crop of tomatoes that cause a spaghetti and meatball party or maybe an apple harvest with cider and pie. Sometimes, there is no reason needed. A Saturday when they are all in town is reason enough. The problem with all of this is the peer pressure that is exerted on each of them to invite their husbands.

"It's Sasquatch!" One guy, Brad. said to me when I showed up at one of these gatherings with Renee. It was a garden party, I guess. It was just them showing off their yard and the new landscaping, but they called the yard a "garden" like we were in England or something.

"Huh?" I asked.

"Well, I am not picking on your beard," Brad said, "But it Is so rare to get a sighting of you at these parties, that most people do not think you exist." Brad chuckled to himself, pleased with the little joke he had made.

"Are you holding your wife's purse?" I asked, "Don't you all know each other? Who is going to steal it? You can put it down on the picnic table, can't you?"

"It is a utility satchel, not a purse."

"Whatever," I said, "You can put it down; what does she have in there that is so valuable?"

"It is mine," Brad said, "And I just like to keep my wallet, checkbook, and cell phone handy. Where do you put yours?"

"My wallet is in my pocket, the phone is in my truck, and the checkbook is in my wallet."

"Oh, I would be interested in a wallet like that; how big is it?"

"Just regular-sized," I said, showing him my wallet, "I just keep one blank check in there in case I need it. Never know when you might find a good deal on a shotgun or something. You carry a whole checkbook?"

"Bob!" Renee grabbed my arm, "I want you to please help me put our casserole on the serving table."

"Did you see Brad's purse?" I asked Renee as we walked to the food table.

We went to a party like this on the Sunday before Thanksgiving.

"Where are we going?" I asked.

"Susan and Jim's place."

"I can't make that," I shook my head.

"We specifically picked a Sunday so that you could make it."

"Are you crazy?" I asked, "I work Sundays."

"Not Sunday afternoons, and you can't hunt on Sundays."

"What is your theme for this shindig?"

"It is a potluck, and I need you to get me a bunch of rabbits this week. Can you get me ten or twelve?"

"Are we feeding everyone?"

"Well, Susan is interested in becoming more free-range in her protein choices. She specifically asked for some rabbit."

"We have that many rabbits in the freezer," I said.

"I just want the back straps for this recipe," Renee said.

"Fajitas?" I asked.

"No, those aren't as good when they get cold. I am making your rabbit stew, but I do not want to risk anyone biting into a small bone. So, all back meat!"

I did a lot of hunting that week and managed to get sixteen rabbits, and while I thought it was a waste not to make fajitas with the tender back straps, I was willing to cooperate.

"Sasquatch!" Brad said when we arrived.

"Dude, I see you have two purses now," I said.

"I still have my utility satchel," he emphasized the word satchel, "And my waist pack holds my battery packs for charging my cell phone and my Fitbit if they get low on power."

"You know that this house has electricity, right?"

"Well, yes, but—"

"You do not want to set your phone down." Let me guess, you charge that phone in the purse, with the cord going down to the battery in the fanny pack?

"Well, yes, but I need to be on alert for work, and I can't have the battery in the phone depleted. What do you do when your phone gets low on power?"

"Last month, the battery died in my truck. I couldn't find it for three days. Finally, my wife located it between the passenger seat and the center console."

"Don't you have a charger in your car?"

"Yeah," I said.

"So, why didn't you use it while driving?"

"I guess I didn't realize it was low."

"Why was it not on your cellphone cradle, on the dash?"

"I don't have that."

"Well," Brad said, "Happy Friendsgiving."

"What?"

Just then, Susan flitted over, "Thank you for making the rabbit stew!"

"Oh, you just let it go in the crockpot; it is pretty easy."

"Those rabbits are all free range?" Susan asked.

"I am not aware of a fence that holds them!" I said.

"Really?"

"I have belonged to many beagle clubs, and I can say that my dogs have gotten outside of the fence at all of those clubs at least once."

"Well, would you offer prayer before the potluck?"

"You all get religion lately? You never have prayer at these things!"

"Well, you have only made two of these meals in the last four years."

"Oh, did the rest have prayer?"

"No, but this is a Friendsgiving feast. It is a low-stress Thanksgiving for friends because you have to eat with your family on Thanksgiving, but this meal can be with the friends who will not be at Thanksgiving because of their own family obligations."

The rabbit stew was a big hit, and the group was pleased with the free-range meat. So, when my wife recently made rabbit stew as a test, I had to ask, "Are we going to one of those Silly Friendsgiving meals again? I never heard of anything so lame. Made up holiday."

"Yes, we are, and we will bring rabbit stew again."

"I think I will be busy."

"Susan's sister got married, and she now has a bed and breakfast. Her husband owned it, and they use it for revenue, especially during home football weekends."

"So."

"We had a gathering there last summer. It is full of rabbits. Susan's sister will be at the Friendsgiving meal. I bet I can get you on that land if you are able to be nice and introduce them to rabbit meat."

"Sounds good!" I said, "When is it?"

"Next Sunday. Oh, and Susan's brother-in-law law, the land-owner, he will be at Susan's house and he always wears his kilt, though it is not a traditional Scottish kilt."

"What kind of kilt is it?"

"Look, here is the thing: it looks just like a skirt, and I know you are going to want to say something. But I think that will not go well for getting you to hunt on that land. Can you just ignore the kilt?"

"How many acres are we talking about at this place?"

Orange Vests & Morning Fog

Halloween, as I remember it, was typically a pretty limited event, meaning it was one night of gluttony and mayhem. Well, as elementary school kids, we also had one day in the classroom where kids got to take a costume, and the teachers got a brief break from teaching in the afternoon while we kids would don our costumes to gather around candy and juice. I'm not sure that the teachers would not have preferred giving instruction rather than being forced to try and contain a couple of dozen kids who are all hopped up on sugar and eager to show off their costumes.

My costume never fit me at school because my mother always bought it (or made it) big enough to be worn over a layer of cold-weather clothing. Or five layers of clothing. Some years, it snowed! Mom was always worried that we would get too cold while we were going door to door, but given the pace of our movement, the more typical problem was sweating too much! It was a mad dash for chocolate, and we knew which houses to visit for the best candy. The problem was that my mother knew all the sweet old ladies in the neighborhood. She knew all the mean old ladies too, but they would turn off the lights in their houses at dark so as not to be bothered with us begging children on their porches.

Mom always made us go to the sweet old ladies' houses when we were really little, and that meant candy corn or worse—you might get a homemade popcorn ball that was rather disappointing. Looking back at our spoiled behavior, I realize that the gals just wanted to try and guess who was in the costume before giving the treats. These silver-haired matriarchs were what passed for a community watch back then, as they would sit on their front porches all year and keep track of every possible movement on their block. If you do something wrong, your parents will find out. The kind of women who routinely swept their sidewalks with a broom and would look with disdain if the neighbors did not do the same.

"Get out there and hose down the sidewalk," my mother once said to me, "Lizzie just called me and told me it was looking dirty." My Mom was in her late 20s then, but the octogenarian named Lizzy was the gal who took care of code enforcement. People who have dealt with the ever-present rules of Home-Owner Groups have no idea what peer pressure can be when you have a Lizzie living next door. Mothers hung back in the dark during trick or treat to not give the older ladies a clue, as Moms knew the fun was in the guessing. Let's face it: the standard procedure was for the homeowner to guess the names of every kid that they could think of until they got the right answer.

I, of course, was always disoriented by the fact that I was running around with fogged glasses, as they would be under the mask—one of those plastic things with a rubber band—and in between houses, I would lift the mask to get my spectacles to defog. Of course, the rubber band eventually broke from all of this, and I would then walk up to a house, holding the mask up to my face with one hand and carrying a sack for candy in the other. Fogged up glasses were simply the nature of Halloween for some of us. Sometimes, if a store requires me to wear a mask for COVID protocols, I get steamed-up glasses, and I sit there with trick-or-treat flashbacks thinking, "Please, no candy corn!"

The kids now have a whole Halloween season to gather candy, and it is not uncommon for them to attend five or six events held throughout the month. Sometimes, they take all the walking out of the affair, and dispense candy bars in a parking lot, passing out candy from the trunks of the vehicles. When the kids do go door to door, they are loaded into a van or SUV and then drive through the neighborhood, pulling into each driveway or along the curb in front of each house, and the costumed marauders disembark from the vehicle like a mechanized infantry unit, swarming to the porch before loading up and driving to the next house with a porch light still shining.

The Day after Halloween is All Saints Day, and in my tradition, that is a day of remembering all believers who passed away, especially those who died within the last year. I, however, tend to go hunting on Halloween and think about all the important people in my life, and much of my life involves hunting with beagles. If I can get into a dense morning fog, deep in a junction of little valleys (hollers) that generate echoes, then I can sometimes feel like I have traveled time. It is odd how a pack of hounds tonguing on a rabbit can mix together in a way that the voices not only merge but can be altered when they begin to rebound through the hills and bounce back at you. You hear the voices leaving, but then they boomerang back through the terrain.

Not too many years ago, I was on such a Halloween hunt, and the morning fog was socked in so tight that I wasn't able to see far enough to get a shot at a rabbit. To be honest, just driving to the spot took a lot longer than it should, one of those fogs where you can't tell if you are driving uphill, downhill, or on the level—unless you take your foot off the accelerator to test it out. I was beginning to wish I had waited until the afternoon to hunt, but they always issue "Dense Fog" advisories, and it is only dense here and there. It was here, there, and everywhere that morning. I dropped the tailgate and unloaded the dog box, turning on the GPS collar of each dog before putting it on the ground. They jumped a rabbit before I got the fourth dog on the ground. Diamond almost squirted out of my hands before I could turn on her collar; she was so anxious to join the chase.

The rabbit crossed the dirt road in front of me—unseen— darting across the narrow lane where I was waiting to get a shot.

To be honest, in my mind, I imagined that it was darting, but it might well have been walking as slow as a tortoise, for all I know. When the dogs got in front of me on the first pass across the road, I looked at the GPS and saw that they were 30 yards in front of me. I could hear them, but I was unable to see them. But they were close enough that the reverberating hound sound lacked the distortion that was characteristic of the echo when they were in the hollow, and I could hear all the dogs distinctly—Duke, Hoss, Diamond, and Blitz. Off they went, running straight up the gully that often drains water under the dirt road, a gully that heads uphill to a stand of the sourest apples I ever brought home. Soon, the pace quickened, and the voices of the baying hounds were bouncing off each other with the echoing topography, and for a Moment, I thought I heard Rebel and Zoe in the mix. I knew that was impossible, as both were deceased. Rebel was Duke's Dad, and Zoe was Diamond's grandmother! But it caught me off guard, and I sat down on a stump to just enjoy the mystical sounds pouring through the mist that really was more like being in a swirl of clouds than morning fog.

They crossed the road again, their voices becoming clear again, and the GPS proclaimed them to be only 15 yards away, and if I am honest, they sounded closer. They thundered down into a sparse stand of pine trees, a cluster of evergreens. It seemed like they were running towards this one area of pines where the trees are spaced so far that the goldenrod skyrocketed upwards within their midst. Then again, given my guessing due to fog, they may have been headed adjacent to that, a spot that has a bit of a clearing. I just couldn't tell from looking at my GPS, so I took it off my neck and slipped it into my game vest. My game vest is getting old. The Orange ain't what it used to be. I suppose the day will come when I get a fine for wearing it—the wrong shade of orange, the legal safety orange having faded as the years have rolled by.

All my dogs take their last ride with that vest. When the old veterans take the last trip to the vet for euthanasia, I let them lie down on it and inhale the odor of all the hunts, all the rabbits, all the hunts, all the memories. I then carry them into the veterinarian's office, often with a different blanket. As I was recalling past hounds, I started hearing them! I heard Shadow and Princess join the chase, and then I heard four dead dogs and none that were currently with me. I slouched off my tree stump and used it for a back rest, listening to a pack that I had not heard in a long time.

They neared my location again, and the echoes were not as resounding as the hounds drew close, and I again heard Duke, Hoss, Diamond and Blitz. They were close enough that I could not be sure that the fog in front of me wasn't also mixed with hot canine breath that was rising with every bark on the hot rabbit scent. The rabbit loped past me. I could see the ears laid back, and he was five or six feet away, ears on a swivel as it disappeared from my sight seven feet away, running right up the middle of the road. The dogs were there soon, and they slowed down a little but kept steady pressure until they pushed far enough that they entered another stand of goldenrod. This time, I heard Princess, the first dog I owned by that name I have repeatedly used. Now I was hearing hounds going back into the 1980s, and I started thinking that I was either delusional, nostalgic, or worse!

I walked back to my truck and got my thermos. I placed my unloaded shotgun next to a stump and plopped down for a hot cup of coffee, happy to hear a pack that had never run together. Then, I heard Duke! But it was the Duke that was my very first beagle, bought in 1985. He had one of those high-pitched voices, and granted, he sounded a lot like my current Diamond dog, but I know that they do not sound exactly alike. Hmm. Then I had two Ladies in there running. A Lady from the 1990s and a Lady who had passed more recently. Actually, Princess was my first Lady's mother. The irony to that is the more recent Lady was the mother to the more recent Princess who was home on the couch when this foggy affair was happening, old and feeble.

As the chase continued, I was more and more content to sit in an atemporal fog of nostalgia and hound music. I saw the rabbit again, this time at 15 feet. The fog was gradually clearing, and I decided I might get ready to shoot. As luck would have it, the chase kept heading out into the distance, which at this point was synonymous with back in time, the odd echo amplifying the memories of past chases. Loop after loop, into the pines and through the goldenrod.

The sun burned through the fog about 10 a.m., and the rabbit stopped on the road, 20 yards in front of me, and stared at me. I shouldered the .410 and prepared to put this spooky rabbit in my vest. Then I thought of the music I had heard and decided to let this rabbit live. I leashed the dogs and thought about the song I had just heard. Ahh, just some strange thing I imagined—preachers can get a little far-fetched or at least too suggestive of the supernatural, right? I got home, and my wife, Renee, asked, "How did it go?"

"Different," I said.

"Get any rabbits?" She asked.

"No."

"That's rare for you; you like one long chase and one rabbit in the vest, as you always say."

"I got the long chase," I sighed.

"You look like something is on your mind."

"I am thinking I may have to stop recycling names for dogs."

As we approach Halloween, I am wondering the odds of that rabbit still being alive. Last spring, Princess took her last ride on the hunting vest. I would like to hear her sing again. Whatever the costumes and candy might say, Halloween is about hope and the timeless love of God.

Dog Days, Rabbit Moons, & Beating the Heat

The dog days of summer aren't named for the tendency of dogs to get lazy in the heat. It is named after the return of Sirius, the Dog Star, which returns in the hottest part of the year (northern hemisphere). It is visible just before dawn. Orion rises in the eastern sky late into the night. Sirius rises even later in the night, right at dawn. When the late summer temps aren't quite as hot as this weekend, I look for Orion and Sirius as I drop dogs to chase rabbits just before daylight. I actually look for them as I load dogs into my truck before I drive them afield. If the sky is bright enough that I can't see both of them, then I left too late. The morning dew will be fading. The great hunter, Orion, absent for months, is now returning as we prepare to enter the hunting season.

Orion has two dogs. Canis Major (named Sirius) and Canis Minor (Procyon is the brightest star and just means before the dog. So, kind of a nameless helper of Sirius). Sirius means scorching. And since Sirius is the brightest star in the night sky, the ancients thought that its rising at dawn with the sun made for the hotter days. Now, Sirius, in terms of constellation placement, is right up against Lepus, the hare. Orion's dogs are chasing the hare. Later myths felt the hare wasn't grand enough, so they have Orion hunting Taurus, the bull, instead. If you are looking at Orion, the hare is below him. Sirius is below him and to the left. The little dog is a bit higher than Sirius and a bit more to the left. Taurus is up and to the right of Orion.

Oh, I'd say hunting hare or rabbit is still viewed as less than epic by most unless you love the hound music. I mean, Sirius may be a sighthound. One myth has him so fast that he can catch anything. The little anonymous dog? I like to think he or she is a scent hound. Finds the hare. Gets it moving. Maybe even underappreciated, just like our beagles who tirelessly track hare and rabbit, while all the big money and attention in national magazines goes to bird dogs, and that is only if they decide to feature small game hunting rather than devote their magazine space to big game. Antlers get people excited. The relentless pursuit of a couple of pounds of meat by tenacious beagles doesn't get the rest of the hunting world too excited. Shoot, if you take the time to price squirrel dogs, you will find that the tree rats garner more attention from the world of hunting dogs than beagles. Seriously, check out the cost of a good squirrel dog. And if you find a dog that trees raccoon all night and squirrels all day? Well, I would have to go to the back to finance the purchase, like buying a car.

No, as August has progressed and I see Orion rising higher into the sky and see the hare and the little hound, I am excited for the changing of the seasons to happen soon. When I was a kid, the changing of the seasons was always foreshadowed by the annual purchase of school clothes. This annual trip of misery was when my mother dragged me to the mall.

Shopping malls were places where you could go and socialize. People walked there in the winter, especially retired folks. There was an entire food court and, on top of that, a restaurant or two. Ohhhh, Mom would walk from one store to another, comparing prices on the same item. You could go to the mall and buy exactly what you wanted that day. There was no two-day wait from Amazon, and you also didn't go to a store and have them tell you that they don't have it in stock, but they could mail it to you. Folks from previous generations were looking at the shopping mall and lamenting the loss of downtown districts, just as some of us now lament the loss of malls.

I was in a mall recently. Most of the stores were gated shut, some empty, others with locked merchandise that you could see through the locked barricades. There was one enclave filled with open stores. It had a place to get a haircut. Oh, and a T-Mobile, AT&T, and a Verizon. Perhaps those cell phone stores are the true source of commercial and social life today. I always dreaded going to the mall. I was one of those kids who spent all his time in the woods. I got a new pair of sneakers that never left the school—lived in my gym locker, and a new pair of boots. I have always worn boots. Heck, I have black leather boots now that I wear to church—they look like dress shoes. I keep them polished, and they are a lot nicer to wear on days when I have a funeral service at a cemetery in the driving rain or slippery snow.

I wore plaid shirts to school most days and blue jeans. When my shirts and jeans got too threadbare, then I was no longer allowed to wear them to school. They were in my closet to use for "play, work, or chores." When I was in college, the "grunge" phase of music became popular. There was a store just off campus selling ratty and tattered denim pants and plaid shirts so that kids could pretend to be Kurt Cobain. They were selling used clothes for more than it cost for new ones! I got a friend to drive me home for my old clothes, and when I walked in, the store owner was goo-goo ga-ga over what I brought.

"This is great, man!" He said, "Are you from Seattle?"

"Nope, just a couple hours north in a rural part of the state," I said.

The return of the school year was a clear indicator that the rising Orion, despite the blazing heat, meant that hunting season and cooler temperatures would soon return! If you are bored enough to try and negotiate the AKC website—it is about the least intuitive website you can encounter—you will find that Pennsylvania, where I live, has a bunch of beagle clubs. Some are NEBGF, some are PBGF, and some are traditional brace. All of the brace clubs were formed when you could hunt with them.

They were hard-hitting gun dogs that were judged by horseback to be able to see the hounds in tall brush. Now, the brace dogs are much slower, and their competitions look for dogs that are not capable of hunting. That trend started about the time I was a kid. One reason that there are so many clubs is that there was a time—not too long ago—when it was illegal to train dogs anywhere else during the summer months. You had to train on club property and were not allowed to chase anywhere else, and one way to ensure that the dogs stayed within the property was to put up fences. It was the quiet season in the wild, as the conventional thinking then was that dogs would destroy all baby rabbits and other newborn wildlife. Biologists have since disproved that mindset, and we can now trail in the wild all year long.

As soon as school started, we would see the hot August days start to cool. It would start with cooler mornings and hot afternoons. Eventually, the daily high temperatures would begin to fall, and I would begin my game of sophisticated hooky. I would go to homeroom, be counted as present, and therefore given credit for the day, then I would sneak away and run home to gather dogs. I could walk my beagles up over the hill from my house and find a hare. It had been a long summer of running inside the fence—and I belonged to a brace club that only tolerated my father and I because we did the work of maintaining the running grounds. Our dogs, in their eyes, were the fastest thing they had ever seen. Ha, sometimes, on those days of hooky, I would get a good chase, pick the dogs up in the late morning, and return to school for the afternoon if I had a test. On other occasions, I would have to hide out all day, dogs tied to a tree, as I had to wait for the school day to end before returning to the yard. I had to make sure my mother didn't see me. I would return home through the backyard and just pretend that I had walked home from school and was merely letting dogs out of the kennel. I was so glad to be allowed to chase in the wild again and even happier to get a big hare that would not go underground after an hour or less, as the cottontails do. The main problem was returning home in my school clothes without getting them dirty or torn, so I often too an old shirt with me, sometimes pants too. I would change under a pine tree the way Superman changed in a phone booth. There are no phone booths anymore, so I'm not sure where Superman changes clothes now, maybe in one of those cell phone stores in the mall. Or under a pine tree.

My wife and I were talking about my hooky skills recently when she commented on my ability to hide. "It seems like I can never find you when it is cool enough to run rabbits. It goes right to voicemail when I call you."

"I am building up my frequent flyer miles," I answered.

"What?"

"I put my phone on airplane mode and just use it as a camera to get pictures of hounds baying on the trail of a rabbit."

Lately, however, there have been no morning chases. When the overnight low temperature is in the 70's, that makes for a very miserable day and very short chases. Ah, the full moon will be coming, and very often, it is shortly after that—the first full moon after Orion and Sirius and the unnamed hound appear—that I will begin running rabbits in the evening, as the days shorten and the evenings get a little cooler. Those evening chases are nice because the dogs have to work a little more than they do on morning dew. If the Greeks saw the hare under the hunter Orion in the constellations, Asian cultures saw the rabbit in the full moon. They didn't see a man in the moon but a hare that was using a mortar and pestle, mixing up the elixir of life. I often think of the rabbit as the elixir of life. Such a small animal that gets overlooked by the big game hunters, but the humble rabbit is preyed upon by everything—weasel, fox, coyote, fox, fisher, mink, hawks, owls, and eagles. Heck, a crow will kill a nest of babies. Use your Google machine to search for "Full moon rabbit," and once you see what is described there, you will never look at the full moon without seeing the hare again. Orion is up, the rabbit moon is coming, and I am about to be very thankful to get out of my basement hovel where I have been hiding from the scorching sun. The hunting season will be here before we know it. The rabbit—a symbol of fertility and life will be pursued as beagles fill the air with hound song. Maybe it is okay that the Greeks never named the little dog. It is my dog. And yours. Happy hunting.

TAILGATING, POWER I, & THE FLYING T

Now that we are entering autumn, I must make a small confession. I do not really pay all that much attention to football. I mean, I watch a few games, but I am not really in tune with the particulars. A prime example of this would be the popularity of fantasy football leagues. Have you ever been trapped in a conversation with someone who has memorized the minutiae of every player in the NFL? If you have not, then consider yourself blessed. Apparently, these fantasy leagues require participants to create a team comprised of players who actually play for real teams but not necessarily on the same team, and then you keep track of the staggering volume of statistics that are generated for each football contest played each week, in order to determine if your imaginary team—comprised of real people—won or lost.

Where I live, most people cheer for The Pittsburgh Steelers. I can't even tell you the names of all their players, let alone the names of all the other players in the country! People are shocked at how little I know about football players. This is not a new problem for me. There is a dog, well known in my part of the world, that went by the name of Nittany Cigar Jackson. He was a field champion, and as the name suggests (Nittany), he was owned by a guy right here in Centre County, Pennsylvania, home of Penn State and the Nittany Lions. Now, here is the thing. When Cigar was making a big name for himself, I knew about the dog, and I knew the owner was named Kenny Jackson.

Shoot, I thought, as I always do, the dog was the more famous part of the equation, not the owner. My friend, Andy Purnell, had his Dead River Kennel, and Cigar is all over the pedigrees of his hounds. Andy has passed away, but all those Dead River dogs on the ground right now—the ones that went through his Dixie dog, all go back to Nittany Cigar. Dixie, incidentally, died of old age on my living room floor not too many years after Andy passed. Anyway, I digress . . .

I had no idea that Kenny Jackson was famous. The reason I did not know, was because I do not pay enough attention to football. He was a star at Penn State, playing wide receiver, and then had a professional career as a wide receiver before retiring and coaching wide receivers at Penn State. It was in those coaching days when Cigar was making a name for himself. I was in college then, but Kenny Jackson belonged to the West Branch Beagle Club and, at that time, wanted a pavilion installed as a place to take shelter in the rain while running dogs. Beagle clubs, as we all know, spend time either being resistant to spending any money or in a hurry to spend it all. I suppose lots of organizations are like that, and the pavilion was not getting built! So, I am told Jackson donated three season tickets to the club to be raffled in a fund-raiser, with the stipulation that part of the proceeds would be utilized to build a pavilion. This was when Penn State was a perennial contender for the national championship and before the Sandusky scandal.

Andy and I spent many hours under this pavilion, looking up the hill as our pack of hounds emerged from the blocks of brush for brief Moments of visibility on the mowed paths before squirting back into the thick cover. We never knew that the pavilion was paid for by the guy who owned the Cigar dog in Andy's pedigrees. Football. I just learned that recently.

Fall sports means hunting for me and football for others. I was recently listening to a gaggle of high school coaches talking amongst themselves at a local eatery. There were a dozen of them or more, and I was standing amongst them, waiting for a table with my wife. "I might run a wishbone!" One said, "Given the kids I have right now."

"I am running no-huddle," another coach said."

"Well, boys," I scratched my beard, pulling on my chin hairs, "I gotta go with an I-Formation or a Power I." I nodded my head in approval with myself, hoping that they would agree.

"Sure," a coach said, "That is standard and common. But you don't have to go with that."

"I like the straight ahead, no wasted motion going left and right, zig zagging of the line. It has always worked for me," I said.

"lateral yards don't count, for sure. The I-formation is Good for sending in plays, too," another coach added, "You never run a wing?"

"It happens," I said, "But it is because my I-formation fell apart."

"What are you talking about?"

"My I-Formation gets too competitive and skirts into a wing formation or even a double wing."

"Buddy," the coach said, "You either run an I or a wing; they don't morph."

"The Flying T bugs me more than the double wing," I said.

"What the hell is a Flying T?" A grizzled, grey-haired coach asked, "I ran the T way back in the day."

"That's when you got four in a power I-Formation," I said, "And then you got six lined up horizontally to the left and six more lined up horizontally to the right."

"Have you lost your mind?" One coach took off his hat in disgust, "You ain't allowed to have more than eleven on the field at once!"

"That's how I feel," I sighed, "Hell, I usually play with just three or four!"

"Hey pal," the grizzled old guy pulled up his trousers by the belt loops, "Where do you coach football?"

"What?"

"What school allows you to coach?"

"Oh," I said, "I thought we were talking about rabbit hunting?"

"Say what?"

"I like an I-formation. All the dogs are on the line. A good Power I is nice when you get wind and that big nose dog can run alongside the line and still get the scent even when not lined up in the I. A wing is the start of bad things as my dogs skirt to get to the front, messing up their assignment, and if we get to the Flying T, well, my dogs are totally off the line. And a bunch of other dogs have joined my team."

"Alright then," the veteran coach patted me on the back, "Is someone here to look after you?"

"I am," my wife, Renee, said to him.

"I hope he gets the help he needs, ma'am."

If that guy doesn't like my offensive schemes, he would hate my tailgating parties. Those are mostly dead rabbits on the tailgate with hunting dogs in the box. I will be leaving my house early on home football weekends at Penn State and returning after kickoff to avoid traffic. The whole town is gridlocked until the game starts, and then you have the roads to yourself. I have a football schedule, just to know what time I should return with my I-formation to clean rabbits. Oh yeah, the tailgate party happens after the game, not before, in rabbit hunting.

BULL PIZZLE AND PIG EARS

"Hey," my wife, Renee, said to me on the phone, "I went to that new pet store in town."

"Oh," I said, while thinking to myself, "How much did this trip cost?"

"Diamond really likes this bull pizzle!"

"Do you know what pizzle is?" I asked.

"No."

"Good," I said, "I will be home soon."

Not only did my wife not know what pizzle is, my spellcheck on the word processor doesn't know the word either, underlining it in red every time it is typed. As you may already know, pizzle is penis. If you are surprised to hear this, you should have seen the shock on Renee's face when I got home, and she was holding a handful of the sticks in her hand, "These things are not cheap, but the dogs love them, especially Diamond!"

"Great," I said, "I will never keep her out of any pasture with a bull or beef steers again. She will be jumping as high as she can, and I will have to protect her from getting stomped."

"What?"

"Bull pizzle is penis," I said, imitating the vocal cadence of Charlton Heston when he said, "Soylent Green is people!" in the movie *Soylent Green*. Apparently, she had never seen the movie and had never seen a good impersonation of Heston before. "Damn you all to hell!" is my other Heston impersonation from the end of *Planet of the Apes* when he realizes he has been on Earth all along. I don't know if Renee has seen that movie, either.

Anyway, she stood there looking at Diamond gnawing away on her prize and then looking at her hand, which held a half dozen pizzle sticks.

"The people at the store said that they were good for cleaning the dogs' teeth. That doesn't seem possible."

"Well, they are very dehydrated."

"I guess so," Renee looked at Diamond, who was flattened out on her belly, holding the treat between her two front paws, and as happy as could be, "She has been working on this for almost an hour."

"Well," I said, "How did you like the new pet store in town?" I was hoping to get an idea of how expensive the prices might be and maybe what the total bill was for the venture.

"I don't care," Renee shook her head, looking at Diamond, "I am still going to buy them…" She tossed the remaining treats down into the plastic shopping bag hastily, as if she was playing a game of Hot Potato, and the music was about to stop! Note: Hot Potato was a game that kids played back in the 1900s before we had handheld video games, cell phones, gaming systems, or money. You can google it.

At any rate, we have been doing our best to clean the teeth on our mutts ever since, paying a lot of money for some extractions. As expensive as this pizzle might be, it can save money in the long run. It is pretty safe, too—if made by a reputable manufacturer because it is easily digested (unlike rawhide), and there are no splinters, like often happens with bones. They are caloric, and that may mean cutting back on kibbles on a day when they are utilized. If my dogs are running hard and burning energy, I don't really worry about the calories, but in the summer months, I will monitor the food intake—I tend to run my hounds less in the summer months, not wanting to injure them in the higher temperatures. There are other ways, and less expensive, to look after the dental health of our hounds, and I use those snacks, too.

I do feed bones to my pooches, though I will be honest: some dogs are not as interested in bones as others. Many vets are apprehensive of bones, but I will use the knuckle bones as a way of removing tartar and keeping the gums healthy. I will get the pet store ones on occasion, but I also will get plain old soup bones from the grocery store, which are cheaper. There is a place near me that sells smoked pork bones for fifty cents! Trust me, that is cheaper than pizzle. I watch them devour the smoked bones and take them away when they get too small. Whether it is pizzle or bones, I usually give them one per week, never more than two. When they are running extensively, I will give them a bone to gnaw one night and maybe a pizzle or even a pig ear on another night of the week.

Pig ears are also beneficial, but some of my dogs just go through them way too fast to get the cleaning benefit on the teeth. During the hunting season, I have had dogs that get one pig ear per day, when the constant chasing allows for the extra calories with ease.

"Want me to give your dog one too?" I asked a friend who was visiting my house with his lab as I doled out the pig ears."

"No, she can't eat those, she gains weight. How often are you feeding those to your beagles?" He asked me.

"The retirees do not get them too much, but some of the dogs that go with me every day get one per day."

"Really?" His eyes widened in disbelief, looking at a 25-pound beagle that was able to thrive on the extra calories because of the increased activity involved in being a rabbit dog that loves his job and gladly does it every day.

"Yep," I said, "And it keeps the chompers clean!"

"Does that get expensive?"

"Depends," I said, "My wife is a good shopper and can find great deals. She gets a bunch when we have a good price somewhere. She gets a lot of them online, often in bulk. That's why we store them in a plastic dog food container with a screw-top lid. Keeps them from going bad or getting broken into by a sneaky dog that gets to them."

That dental health translates to more than cheaper vet bills and not paying for tooth extractions. Makes for a better nose, too. Bad teeth can affect the sense of smell. Senses and how they work are fascinating aspects of life. Butterflies see more colors than we do—they see runways on flowers that guide them to the nectar in the center. Predators, including humans, have binocular vision (our eyes are together on the front of our head), which enables the ability to time attacks, determine distance, and maximize the benefits of depth perception. Prey species have their eyes on the sides of their heads, and since we are all about the bunnies, it is not a surprise to any of us that a rabbit can see nearly 360 degrees around itself and can see above their heads, too! Our binocular vision gets about a 190-degree field of vision and nothing above us.

When I get a stuffy nose, I like to eat hot spices on pasta, mustard on cold cuts, and horseradish on roast beef. Why? Because when it drains my sinuses, I can taste better. We have all had sinus congestion that makes food seem tasteless. Taste and smell are connected, and improved dental health keeps a dog's sense of smell working optimally. Tooth decay wafts up to the nose, and it may be that a dog loses some scenting ability as it ages.

There are lots of things about scent that baffle me. Moisture is good for scent, but some days, a light rain that should increase the scent seems to hinder the pack (of course, a deluge will often make the scent worse, but not always). Under certain snow conditions, I swear the scent smells better when it is old as if the rabbit leaves a track and it stirs up the granulated snow to melt—and the older tracks have melted more than the freshest ones, and that melting gives a stronger scent. People get all worked up about barometric pressure and what it may or may not do to the scent, and all of those things are fascinating and confusing to me at the same time.

One thing I do know is that dental care helps. Pizzle. Bone. Pig ears. I have bought those cow hooves stuffed with rock-hard cheese or peanut butter. I avoid rawhide due to concerns of big bits of the rawhide causing blockages—it ain't as digestible as the pizzle. Sometimes, when I need the dogs to be especially quiet while I am working, I will take them to my basement office and let them worry away a knucklebone while I am on the phone. In the winter, I will sit by the wood pellet stove down there in our subterranean den and let the hunting house hounds enjoy the reward of a bone after a good hunt. I find myself listening to the muffled sounds of chewing and canine coos of contentment. I then think about the chase and the mystery of scent as those teeth are being cleaned. I am always happy to learn something new about scent.

One of the things I recently discovered was that having two nostrils isn't a coincidence. When I learned this, it was suggested that I smell my coffee with one nostril only, pinching the other one shut. Then, smell the coffee again with the other nostril. I will let you do that now. Did you do it? Ain't that weird?! Two different scents! Wild, ain't it? I bet you have the same look on your face right now that my wife did when she learned what is used to make pizzle sticks.

In the Woods

"I'll be back," my wife said as she set her phone on the table and wheeled around to go to the restaurant's restroom. The waitress flitted by and asked, "Need a refill?"

"Sure," I said, and get my wife a third glass of the carbonated water and lime." Then, the table started buzzing. This is pretty typical whenever my wife's phone is on a table. I looked and saw that it was a phone call from Wesley, our son. Well, he's my stepson. That was established early in our relationship after I married his Mom.

"I told my Dad that I call you Dad, too," Wes said to me when he returned from a weekend visit.

"Yeah? How did that go?" I asked.

"He doesn't want me to do that. He got mad."

"Well, just make life easy and call me something else."

"How about if I call you Bob?"

"That works fine with me. I've already been trained to answer to that name."

Two months later, Wes came home from his Dad's house and said, "Dad got mad again."

"What went wrong?"

"He was calling me to the kitchen, and I said, "I'll be there in a minute, Bob! He was mad I did not call him Dad." He was nine years old then. He is 26 now.

Anyway, the buzzing table went to voicemail, and my phone, in my shirt pocket, started buzzing.

"Yeah," I answered, seeing it was Wesley.

"Hi Bob," he said in his baritone monotone, "Do you know where Mom is?"

"She is in the bathroom," I said, "What's up?" I could almost guess what was up—he was looking for some money.

"I am playing a few gigs soon, and I need some money."

"Where is your paycheck?"

"Well, Bob, if I still had that money, I wouldn't be calling you."

"Alright, bud, stop by the house. I have a few jobs I could pay you to do."

"Can't I just get what I need and pay you back?"

"Only if you give me your debit card, and I will get the money in cash when your direct deposit paycheck clears before you spend it all on video games and pizza."

"Okay," the monotone came through the phone, "I will come over tomorrow after work."

"Get there before it rains; scooping dog dirt in the yard is better before it liquifies," I gave him a little encouragement.

Renee heard that last part as she sat down, "Aren't you worried that you will hurt his self-esteem by making him clean poop?" Much of modern life is concerned with self-esteem. I have never understood this obsession, but my father was more concerned that a person would have too much self-esteem rather than not enough. "Confidence doesn't need affirmation, and it doesn't need to brag," he would say.

"If he gets there too late," I said to my wife, "I will already have it scooped, and there will be less work he can do. And my self-esteem will be fine. I have been picking up turds for, well, how many years? Since 1985 . . ."

Nostalgia hit me, and I was back in 1985 with my first beagle. Back then, sawdust was free. Any store that sold lumber had free sawdust. Dad got it in a giant burlap sack from the local building supply center. We had an outdoor kennel with wire runs and a cement slab underneath. Every day, rain, shine, sleet, or snow, I was out there with an old metal coffee can that was filled with water, Pine-sol, and a toilet brush. I would scrub the wire with the brush and knock the feces to the sawdust that covered the cement slab below. The sawdust collected urine, too. I then got a hoe and drug all the sawdust out, and I then shoveled the sawdust into a big metal can lined with the extra heavy-duty garbage bag. Lastly, I scattered fresh sawdust under the wire runs of the kennels. Every. Single. Day. The garbage bag went to the end of the driveway each week on garbage night. I scrubbed so much wire with Pine-sol that I cannot use it in my house. Renee mopped with it when we first got married. I took a whiff and, full of nausea, said, "Can we please never use Pine-sol again? I know it is a great product, but all I smell is dog-shit when people use it!"

Wood pellets, which are made from sawdust, cost over $4 per bag last winter. I figure I shoveled enough sawdust as a kid to pay for a new truck at modern sawdust rates! After cleaning kennels, I could walk over the hill from my house and jump hare or cottontail to run, and that was one of my favorite things to do as a kid. Whenever anyone asked, "Where is Bob?" My Mom would say, "If them dogs ain't in the yard, then he is in the woods."

"In the woods" was the term used for everything from camping to fishing to making tree forts or just walking. We didn't have hiking. Hiking is what people do when they drive to the woods before they start walking. When you live in the woods or right next to them, then it is just called going for a walk. "The woods" had been timbered, mined for coal, and timbered again over the years. My Dad had a deer stand on a spot he called the clear-cut. The "clear-cut" was covered with tall trees about 20 inches in diameter, so how long ago was it a clear-cut? At some point in my father's life, it was definitely timbered, but it wasn't recent! I was 30 years old before I even considered the fact that my Dad lived his entire life within a mile of the house where he was born, except for a couple of years in the Philippines during the Second World War. He spent 60 of his 64 years within 100 yards of those same woods that I roamed every day.

Dad grew up on those same acres. As a kid, he climbed a tree and beat the crows away to get a hatchling. He fed it, and it was trained to roost in the yard and flew down to his shoulder when he would go outside. It even said a few words from time to time. In those same woods, as a kid, he carved his name on a flat rock with a hammer and chisel.

"Where is that rock?" I asked.

"Somewhere on the edge of Gordon's pasture. The Gordon farm also bordered the woods. I can't tell you how many times I looked for that rock, and I am sure that it got tilled over as the pasture and fields were moved and adjusted. Being chased by the Gordon's bull was almost a daily occurrence for me if I had dogs out and they bounced a cottontail in the fallow field. The bull would get aggravated at the dogs, and I would rush in like a rodeo clown to give it a bigger target. I see people with arm tattoos that look as if barbed wire is running around the circumference of the bicep. I have had barbed wire around my arm as I was diving out of the cow pasture—I wished I had a barrel for an escape. Speaking as a guy who has had actual barbed wire on me, I have no desire to get a tattoo of the stuff. Being around barbed wire makes you not want it on your arm! In my youth, I much preferred chasing the hare; they never went in the farm but stayed in the woods, no need to see that bull.

I was looking for that rock again not too many years ago and decided that it was gone forever. I sat next to a dead log and carved my name into it. That log will definitely decay into nothing if it hasn't already.

In the 1950s, Dad had beagles, and he would open the kennel door at his house and turn them loose in the woods next to the Gordon farm—A very short walk. If he had to go to work at three, he would leave, and the dogs would come home eventually. One day, his beloved Prince dog never returned.

"I saw the dog with your brother, Clarence," a guy told my Dad, "He was hunting the bottom fence row."

Dad found the dog dead; shot. He felt Clarence killed the dog out of jealousy because it was a far better hound than any Clarence had. I hate to think someone would be that cruel to anyone, let alone a sibling. I think it was just as likely that Clarence shot at the rabbit when the rabbit was first jumped, and Prince was too close. He left the dog lay, not wanting to tell Dad. That's just my hunch. At any rate, Dad got out of beagles right after that and never got another until 1985, when I begged for one.

I was allergic to dogs my whole life. A friend had a beagle, and we would take it out all the time into the same woods. I was hooked and wanted a dog. I remember praying every night to no longer have allergies to dogs. Then, we figured out that dogs no longer bothered me. We were in my cousin's house one day, a cookout got rained upon, and we went inside with the intent to eat and leave before my allergies flared up. We stayed for hours with no problems! My cat allergies never went away; I still have them to this day. I still get stuffed up in a barn with horses or cattle. A friend has goats—yep, they make me sneeze and snot, too. Dog allergies are gone. But Dad and I got beagles and built the kennel. I probably spent more time with those beagles in the woods than I did with any single friend as a kid. Guys will often pay someone to start a beagle puppy or pay someone to condition dogs or take them to trials. I never minded the solitary hours of being with dogs and listening to the chase. It always allowed me to think and relax. They were always enough company for me, and to this day, I tend to hunt rabbits by myself. I don't need lots of conversation interfering with the hound music. I was probably conditioned to be like that as a teenager when all my friends were more interested in sleeping in on summer mornings and fixing cars in the afternoon. I just went to the woods. I couldn't afford a car, so I ran dogs and then would beg Dad for his truck. Once in a while, he would let me take it out on a date.

One day, Dad and I watched our beagles—his Princess and my Duke, running a rabbit, and he said, "Thanks for getting me back into beagles." He said it matter-of-fact, looking at the dogs, not me.

"I had to beg enough!" I said. Princess was named as an homage to his Prince dog, whom he found dead decades earlier. My Dad was 45 years old when I was born, so it was like being raised by a grandfather. I have half-siblings old enough to be my parents. I have nephews and nieces older than me! The decades between Prince and Princess seemed to fade away for my father, and it was like he always had dogs. Dad and I were always in the woods. We bred Princess and got a couple more pups. I often wondered how different my life would have been if I had remained allergic to dogs. What if a person born to be a florist was allergic to flowers, or a guy born to be a carpenter was allergic to wood?

Ten years ago or so, I was tested for allergies, and my back was pricked with all those needles. It itched right away.

"I hope you don't go outside," the allergist said.

"Why?" I asked.

"You are allergic to every tree, bush, grass, or any plant pollen! Your back must itch."

"Oh yeah," I said, "And don't forget cats. My lungs get wheezy within minutes of being in a house with cats."

"Yes, and dogs too," he said.

"What?"

"You are as allergic to dogs as you are cats!"

"That must be a false positive," I said.

"No, you are definitely allergic to dogs. But the good news is you are no longer allergic to seafood of any kind or eggs. You outgrew those allergies." That was why I was getting tested.

"I must have outgrown dog allergies, too."

"Nope, I wouldn't get a puppy if I were you." I didn't bother to tell him I was living in a house with a half dozen rabbit-running, brush-busting beagles.

I was thinking about that earlier and remembering how much I prayed to get that first beagle. I remember how the hound song changed my whole life. Especially the last summer Dad was alive. I was a college freshman and home for a few months before starting my sophomore year. I was running Duke and Princess while he was in the living room, gooned out of his mind on narcotics as cancer ravished his body. While listening to those dogs, I decided to study things that were more philosophical and theological. Science and math had always been my jam. My high school even created an advanced physical sciences course, I was the only student. I had exhausted every other science class available, there were none left for me to take. I was left, unsupervised, in a lab to do experiments every day. I was top-heavy in math and science in my first year of college, too, and I loved it. My work-study job was in the chemistry laboratory.

"Dr. Clippard," I said, "Our lab in class today is to determine the molarity of this sulfuric acid."

"Yes, I know. I gave the assignment."

"Umm, I mixed this solution at work this morning. I already know the answer."

"Oh, well then, you shouldn't be here long."

The day Dad mentioned his return to beagles, Duke and Princess brought that rabbit out of the pasture, down past the bottom fence row where Dad had found Prince's lifeless body, and went up to the top again, and I decided right then and there that I was no longer wanting to study the notions of how the world came into being, but the so what of creation. We have this great world, so how do we live in it? Names carved in wood are ultimately as ephemeral as names chiseled in stone. The lives that go with the names can have a real impact—good or bad—on the people around them. The folks who are hikers and see the woods as a place far away are ultimately as connected to those natural places as those of us who live in the middle of them.

I would never pay someone to start a puppy, not that I am judging anyone else for doing it. There is just something about that the first time a pup barks on rabbit scent. It makes a bark that he has never bayed before. It doesn't sound like a playful bark with other pups, nor does it sound like an angry bay at an intruder or rival. It is a dog's rabbit voice, and it truly is like a switch going off in their little brains, and they are activated and will never be the same. From that moment on, their primary focus is rabbits. The pup has answered a calling.

"We aren't out of the woods yet" is something people often say as if the woods were a place to be avoided or a bad place. More and more, I find myself going into the woods and not wanting to get out of them.

"You know that, right?" my wife said, drawing me out of nostalgia at the restaurant and snapping me back to the present.

"What?"

"Wesley needs a guitar."

"I bought him two guitars over the years," I said.

"His electric guitar got stolen."

"Oh, I didn't know that." I was stingy about buying him junk, but I always supported his musical talent, and he is very good.

"Is he going to make enough money scooping poop to get a guitar?"

"Tell him I will buy the guitar if he scoops the poop and also goes in the woods."

"What woods?"

"The woods," I said, "They are all fundamentally the same, on a primal level. He needs to hear a beagle's rabbit voice and learn what it means to answer a calling."

"You say some strange things when you come out of those trances."

"I will make him run dogs. And listen to them. He won't want to do that, but I will have him do it to pay off the debt. He can catch dogs for me, too, if the pack splits and we have dogs on two different rabbits." Wes used to like the woods, but as a teenager, he turned into a suburbanite.

"He will probably get lost!"

"I will put a tracking collar on him too," I said, "And you can pay for this supper!"

GROWING UP

May. It is about Mother's Day in so many ways. I feel as if I have told so many stories over the years about how great my Mom was to me and how supportive she was in everything I did. I suppose I have told the stories about her support of my beagling the most, at least in print. But she was my biggest fan in all things. I thought that this month, I would talk about my low points as a son. I guess I will start with applying to college. Back then, Penn State was an affordable college for a working-class kid (don't look at the tuition today). By the time I went to college, I knew my life had gone to the dogs. Penn State has a bunch of branch campuses, and the closest one to my hometown was Dubois. The Mom grapevine had sufficiently convinced my mother that Penn State Dubois was the party Mecca of the universe, and she decided that I should not go there. Hell, I was willing to go as a commuter, and the money I would have saved in dormitory costs would have more than paid for a junky jalopy to get me there! Ah, but the stories of the parties in Dubois made Mama worry. So, she had me apply to the main campus, of all places! That place made Dubois look like a monastery!

One visit had me terrified. Not the parties, but the size of the place was intimidating. I think it was 40,000 students then! So, after much begging, I convinced the university to let me go to my second choice, which was the Altoona campus.

"You were accepted at the main campus!" The officials wailed, "Why do you not want to come here? Most kids would do anything to start here?"

"I really wanted to go to Dubois," I said. This really boggled their minds, as Dubois was a very small campus, right next to the high school in town. Altoona was pretty big for a branch campus, and that is where I went to start. University Park, the main campus, was so big that I felt intimidated by the number of students. The campus was bigger than my town. It was a dreadful thought, going to Altoona, being away from home, and not running dogs. Dubois would have suited me fine; I could run dogs, take classes, and get along just fine with the students who also hailed from rural, north-central Pennsylvania.

On move-in day, I remember being less than happy. Granted, my best friend, Joe, was going to Altoona too, but I was probably one of the few kids who could have been happy commuting and not really having the "college experience" of moving out. All the kids said, "I love you" to Mom and Dad, and parents went home. A few weeks later, I was home for Labor Day, and Dad said, "All those other kids told their Moms that they loved them, and you did not."

I did not grow up in a house where people said "I love you" that much. Sure, we all knew it and felt it, but it wasn't vocalized. Not unless it was serious stuff—like surgery or a terrible accident and you were going into the emergency room! I say it to my wife and stepson all the time now, but that was not the way things were in my childhood house. Looking back, I remember all those new college students with tears, saying goodbye with love. What were my thoughts? I was thinking, "Great, I am in Altoona, a city, and my dogs are hours away."

I got home a few weekends that first semester, and I hunted rabbits hard. Dad was dying from cancer, though we didn't know it. He had beaten cancer years before, and it had returned, but the doctors were treating him for back problems, unaware that the disease had advanced with a vengeance. Dad kept working, wincing with pain and even rabbit-hunted with me. I kept thinking it would be so much easier if I were in Dubois. Oh, by the way, comparing Dubois to Altoona, in terms of parties, is like comparing traditional brace dogs to SPO dogs.

And comparing Altoona to the main campus is like comparing UBGF SPO to LPH!

I only went for two years to Altoona and had to transfer to the main campus to complete my degree. Dad had died, and Mom was working a lot of hours but would come to get me for a few hunting trips. I was in an apartment with five other roommates, and it was a college apartment! Kegs. Messes. All that stuff. Not a pleasant thing for Moms to see. I went home to see her whenever I could catch a ride. At home, I would run dogs in the places where Dad and I always did, almost hearing his voice. Well, one dog. We had some good hunting dogs, and Mom sold all but my old Duke dog. She was making minimum wage at a convenience store after Dad died. I understand it now, especially since she got so much money for Princess, Dad's dog. Her pups sold well, too. I was out hunting hare over Christmas break, and old Duke was slowing down. I stayed out until almost dark, waiting until I could shoot a hare in our limited Pennsylvania season. I could have gone home sooner, but I was bitter about the young dogs being sold. Hindsight being what it is, I know it was for the best and those dogs had a much better life running rabbits all year rather than waiting for me to get home on sporadic weekends.

None of this is to say I was angry or mean. I was just in flux—a full-time student, not knowing where I was headed. I graduated college and went straight to seminary, which made everyone in the family confused! I guess I was always a bit rebellious, at times a hothead, and definitely not always gregarious or good at small talk. But I was thinking about the big questions—life, death, eternity, the meaning of life, and all those things that are part and parcel of life in ministry. What do I remember about graduation from Penn State? Not wanting to go. It is a mostly impersonal affair at a school that big, and I was happy to let them mail my diplomas. Mom and Grandma wanted to attend. So we attended. I was sullen and silent. My mind was focused on the fact that I had earned a couple of degrees that were not really good for the job market until I went to seminary and finished. I regret not being happy. I had some relatives who had gone to college, but I don't know that any with the last name of Ford had done it. Shoot, to be honest, a lot of the Fords in my family are smarter than me—mechanics, electricians, carpenters. I was the nerdy kid with a good memory and not much skill.

"Good thing you're strong," Dad would say, "You got two options—unskilled labor, which is not going to be around much longer—or those book smarts. Skilled craftsmanship is not your thing!" I have relatives that can restore cars, build houses, and build roads. I once replaced a faucet handle without flooding the house, and I thought I was really being a handyman. Mom was happy at graduation, and I should have been too.

I was a student pastor in seminary and had a beagle. The one old beagle I had back home had died, and I got a new one. It stayed at a church member's farm. Rural place outside of town. By then, Mom got a secretarial job in a construction company. I still remember the last time I saw her. I went to see her in Texas for Easter. The church I was serving told me to go and gave me the Sunday off! No church does that, but they knew I wanted to see my Mom, and I was a student. Mom and I went to the sunrise service; not many were there in attendance. She died the following August. Her body was shipped back to Pennsylvania. I ran my dog at the farm near my seminary for three solid days before I went to the funeral.

I wish I would have officiated the funeral. I thought I would get too emotional. The pastor put zero effort into the service. Never learned a thing about my Mom. It was nothing but bare-bones liturgy. Prayers and scripture. He had to think hard to remember her name for the few times he had to mention her. That night, I went to my childhood home and, in the quiet darkness, offered the service that I should have done. No one was there but me in the stillness of my backyard. I will never be too emotional to officiate a funeral again. I learned a trick that night. When

I get too emotional to talk, I bite the inside of my cheek until it bleeds, driving away the tears. I've used that same technique at funerals to bury childhood friends, fellow beaglers, beloved church members, and mentors. It looks like a pregnant pause, an oratorical tool, but it is the internalization of grief to carry on—blood and saliva mixed. Oh, and I have never done a shoddy funeral, not even for a stranger. I learn a little something, as best as I can. I personalize them all.

Ah, I have written a lot of stories about my Mom that show how wonderful she was, how much I loved her, and how much she loved me. Why did I write this one? Just to show that things in families can be bad at times, but love still reigns. And when it seems like nothing good can ever happen, it does, like that Easter in Texas. My Mom asked me what my Easter sermon would have been. I told her the gist of it and explained that I would deliver it the next Sunday when I returned to that little church in Ohio next to that seminary.

"Where did you get those thoughts?" she asked.

"Running this beagle, I have there and thinking," I answered.

"Are you mad I had to sell all but the one beagle?" She asked.

"Of course not," I said, "I love you." I was no longer hesitant to speak of love.

"Keep listening to those beagles," she said.

Pussy Willows & Chocolate Eggs

You know how they say that it is cliché to get your wife flowers or chocolate? I can tell you that getting my wife, Renee, some chocolate is a guaranteed way to get her happy or get me out of trouble. I mean, don't get me wrong, chocolate will not prevent me from getting in trouble, but it can lessen the amount of time when I am being ignored, blasted with eye rolls, or dismissed. I would not say that Renee really yells. But when she is upset, she will just be snarky and end a conversation.

"Hey, hon," I said once, "Do you think it would be okay if I go hunting on Saturday?"

"Oh," she rolled her eyes, "I wasn't aware that you started asking what I thought. Last Saturday you just woke up early and left the house with dogs, even though I had told you I made plans."

"Yeah," I said, "I thought you meant that you made plans for you, not for us. Something that you were going to do alone."

"Whatever," she snarked, turned on her heels, and looked at me over her shoulder with an eye roll so convulsive that it left her mouth open in order to tell me that she was calling me a mouth breather with questionable intelligence and no ability to remember "plans" that had been made. Perhaps, as a reader, you sympathize with me, and maybe you are rolling your eyes in complete agreement with Renee. The reality was that I had been found guilty in my "court-marital." A "court-marital" is like a court-martial insofar as it is a legal process with distinct differences from other legal proceedings that most people face. Renee is both the prosecuting attorney and the judge in the court-martial. I get no legal representation. There is no jury—the judge determines guilt and innocence (I presume that innocence is a possible result; I have just never seen it happen). In fact, guilt could be summarily determined without a prosecutor. Renee's prosecutorial role, I think, is to educate the defendant (me) about where he went wrong. Plus, I think she enjoys presenting timelines of my malfeasance and hypothesizing on motivations for my crimes.

"You see, she once said, "You intentionally let those wet beagles run across my freshly mopped, and still damp, kitchen floor in order to get mud on it."

"Um, I didn't know the floor had been mopped."

"So, you think muddy paws are okay if the floor was totally dry when you got home from the woods?"

"I don't think that is wh—"

"Exactly! You don't think!"

"Yes, your honor."

"I'm the prosecutor right now, not the judge."

But a sentence can be lightened. Not by an appeal to a higher court or anything so logical. It is good old-fashioned bribery, just like the real legal system! Oh, I pick blackberries in August and will catch some brook trout in the spring, but the year-round bribe that always works is chocolate. Renee eats chocolate in tiny but daily amounts. Just a tiny bit, is all. I learned this about a year into our marriage when Wesley, my stepson, was still living at home. Where Renee would eat a tiny bit of chocolate, Wes was able to gulp it down in copious quantities. My wife would stock a jar with M&Ms, and Wesley would wake up and call that jar his breakfast. That is when I saw it happen—Renee walked into the office and, in the back of a drawer, grabbed a Hershey Kiss. Just one, at the end of the day, when Wes had eaten all the other candy that morning.

"What did you do?" I asked.

"That's my emergency chocolate," Renee said, "For when the rest has been inhaled by the gluttons!" One small bite of chocolate destroys stress for her.

I can't even tell you what chocolate I use as bribery. I just go to Wegman's and get something expensive and often imported. Oh, and close to Easter, I will get her the Cadbury Eggs—she only likes the Caramel. They are the perfect size for a bribe that gets the wheels of justice rolling to lessen my sentence in marital court. I stock up on them at Easter time. And now, there is a new item to get in Spring—pussy willows. Let me explain.

Last Spring, there were no palms available for Palm Sunday. Nada. Zilch. The country was shut down for Covid, and that is when I learned that the Orthodox churches in our area, and also some Roman Catholic Churches, would celebrate with pussy willows instead of, or in addition to, the traditional use of palms. This is an old tradition in Europe, dating back to when it wasn't easy to get Palm branches to Northern Europe without a lot of trouble and cost. The tradition was brought to America. Now, I can tell you I heard about this last year and thought it was a great idea, especially since I knew a spot where I would see them growing at a location where I frequently run dogs. I went there every day with a pack of beagles, at first struggling to find the willows. Once I located them, I kept returning, waiting for them to bloom. It is the white blooms that are appealing; there would be no point in gathering a bunch of twigs. Pussy willows are one of the first plants to blossom and therefore represent new life and renewal.

As a Beagler, the willows had even more meaning for me— the bark from the young willows is a favorite food source for rabbits when the snowpack has covered the grasses and clover. When they bloomed last year, I cut a few branches. Renee was so ecstatic that I got her a few more, and she put them in various food coloring to change the blossoms into a dazzling array of colors. I was just checking out this year's crop of pussy willows the other day in a patch of rabbit cover where snow still covers the ground on the north-facing slopes of the hills. The rabbits feasted hard on both the Sumac and the willow bark this winter.

We got a big snow in mid-December and never saw bare ground in my hunting spots until the first week in March—and that has been sporadic and south-facing. I am waiting for the willows to blossom, and this recent warm weather has blasted the snowpack and is doing its best to coax Mother Earth into revival after the winter chill has begun to recede and the ground has gone from frozen to muddy. Speaking of mud, I had another court-martial. I did my best to keep the beagles off the floor. A beagle paw gets muddy. When it dries, it becomes, well, dirty. Now, that dirt will leave mud on a wet floor, so I now have to clean the paws at my truck when the chase is over. Yeah, I take a jug of soapy water and a wash rag, and I clean each paw before putting each dog back into the dog box. Do you have any idea how embarrassing it is for your friends to catch you at this? This is not normal beagle club behavior!

It was all going so well until I made a recent pussy willow check. I opted to take Renee's little car to save gasoline and just took one dog, Diamond, because I was going to be stopping at the office for a couple of hours and needed a dog that would just sit in the corner and be lazy, not a pack playing rough house in the parish office. My wife had Zoom meetings all day for work, she never knew I took her car, put more than 90 miles on it, and saved gas money compared to using my Tacoma.

"Can I talk to you?" Renee said a couple of days later. That is the court-martial equivalent of "All rise!"

"Sure," I said, sounding calmer than I was.

"Have you had beagles in my car?"

"Sure, you know beagles have been in there; I couldn't name each and every occasion since you got that particular car."

"I mean recently," she said.

"Jeez," I scratched my chin, "Not today or anything like that."

"This month?"

"Hmm," I looked pensive, "In the last 30 days? I mean, maybe. Yes, I think so. For sure, I went hunting in mid-February; remember, you went too. We went out east to meet people with less snow."

"Yes, I remember," she slammed an eye roll jab followed by a dismissive hand wave of a hook, "But I mean this month, This calendar month."

"Oh, the last eight days? Hmmm. Yeah. I did."

"Apparently, you used no crates; my windows are covered in smears from the noses of dogs!"

"That's not true," I stated emphatically.

"So, you used crates?"

"Oh," I feigned surprise, "Sorry, I did not use crates."

"So," her eyes rolled so deep I worried she might walk around without visible pupils for a week, "What are you saying is untrue about what I said?"

"The smears from the noses of dogs. You said dogs. It was just one dog. Not plural."

"Was it your spoiled little Diamond?"

"It was," I said.

"Did she, after getting my windows dirty, sit in the front passenger seat?"

"Yes," I said, "How did you know?"

"I picked up my mother to take her for a doctor's appointment," the prosecutor thundered, "And it was raining. She got a little wet using her walker to get to the car."

"Yes, I am familiar with the concept of rain," I said, coming dangerously close to being found in contempt of court.

"Your wet rabbit dog must have dried off in the seat, depositing a layer of dust, which got wet again when Mom sat down!" Her eyes went white, not like a standard eye roll, almost like a zombie.

"I think rehydrated is the proper language."

"Call it what you want, but she went in with white pants and a muddy bottom." Her hands went to her hips to signify that guilt had been ascertained.

Well, if you will excuse me, Palm Sunday and Easter are approaching. But I think I am going to look for some early blooming willows and see if they sell those eggs that the Easter Bunny lays by the case.

Goats & Dogs: A Tale of Romance

Valentine's Day is coming soon. I always struggle to decide what my wife will want for the special day. What I mean by a special day is one with scary origins that has become even scarier in modern times. Pre-Christian Romans had a festival in mid-February called Lupercalia. They went to a cave where they believed two orphaned babies (the founders of Rome) were raised by a wolf that gave them milk. At the cave they would sacrifice a goat to encourage fertility and also a dog for purification. Now it gets more weird.

They would tear the goat hide into strips and soak it in blood. These blood-soaked chunks of goat hide would then be used to slap things like fields and orchards to encourage fertility. Oh, and women. Yep. They would slap women with bloody goat hide to encourage fertility. These bachelorettes lined up for this, which is quite different than our day and age, where home pregnancy kits are sold in the hopes that infertility has prevailed.

Anyway, all the recently blood-spattered maidens put their name in a hat (okay, it was some ceremonial pottery or something), and the single guys in town would randomly pick one of the names and take the gal home for a year. They often then married. All of this was done, I presume, because they did not have the internet to find a suitable marriage partner online, which I think is how people get married now if the commercials are true. After Rome had lots of Christians, the Church decided to put an end to the Bloody Goat Hide Day and replaced it with Valentine's Day. There are no less than three guys by this name that could be the saint who gave his name to the day, and they all got killed. Somehow, this all leads to modern ideas of romance, but I am not sure how that occurred. My research department (a friend with high-speed internet) did not answer my call, or I could tell you. Myself, I had to meet my wife, Renee, in person, which is how we get to the scarier part of the holiday—romance today!

My wife and I attended the same seminary, and she tells everyone about the first time we ever met. She will start by saying, "I couldn't stand him and thought he was the rudest person I ever met." Let me explain how this love-not-at-first-sight happened. I worked in the maintenance department, and she worked in the library. I had impressed my boss with my great honesty. By honesty, I mean I had kind of wrecked the truck. Not really, but I was trying to back up to the dumpster to unload rotted drywall that we had replaced, and in my attempt to get really close to the receptacle managed to scrape the entire side of the truck.

The truck, to be fair, was covered in dents, scratches, and other blemishes.

"Gene," I said, "I just put a scratch in the truck,"

"Bobby, that's okay."

"It's a big one. I have it parked outside the office here."

"Well, I am sure it isn't that bad," Gene started walking for the door to investigate, "It will just blend in with all the other— holy crap, did anyone get hurt in that collision?!"

"No. But the dumpster moved a little."

A few weeks later, Gene approached me and said, "You are the first person to admit to damaging the truck. Ever. All the full-time guys drive it, and you students, too. Everyone always denies it and hopes I don't notice. Or hope that by the time I do notice, there is no way to determine what happened."

"I wouldn't feel right about doing that," I said.

"Well," Gene sighed, "Yours was hard to miss. Anyway, as the first honest student I have had, I want to give you keys to the whole campus. You can reset the fire alarms when they go off after five p.m. during the week days and all day on weekends. I will pay you an hour every time you turn off the alarm because people burn supper and the smoke alarm rings. Also, I will pay you an hour's pay every night to lock up all the buildings on campus."

It only took 15 minutes to reset the alarms. It seems the only thing rarer than an honest maintenance worker at that place was a good cook. I was always getting called at supper time to reset the alarms, but in everyone's defense, they were sensitive alarms. Locking up the public buildings at night could take longer—especially if the student in charge of the library had not yet gotten the library prepped to be locked. Renee was never ready. Ever. That is all I remember about that, but apparently, according to her, I said things like, "Are you ever on time for things? How much longer before I can lock up? Is this going to take long? You still aren't ready?"

I don't recall those "snide" comments that she claims I made, but I say them to her all the time now. Years later, we got married as pastors serving different congregations. I need to get her a gift every year at this time, and I don't think a fresh dab of goat blood will do. Renee currently works at the university, and I was sending flowers there so that all the gals in her office could see them being delivered. This was a recommended gift idea from a florist. It turns out that this floral delivery causes conflict in the workplace between the "haves" and the "have-nots" in terms of flower recipients. The real reason I don't do it, though, is that you have to remember to order them before February 14 because they always get too busy or sell out of the "good" flowers. In this case, good means outrageously expensive rather than garden variety expensive.

Chocolate is a gamble. If you are married, you understand this, and if you are single, you will understand someday. Small bits of chocolate are good throughout the year, but large quantities as the sole gift can be misunderstood. For now, I will tell you that when a woman gets chocolate and says, "What are you saying by giving me this?" there is no correct answer. None. I am going with a gift card from the massage place in the local shopping mall this year. In part, this is my being selfish because every night, she wants me to rub her neck, stretch an arm, or push my heel against her hip. I am not sure what goes down at her massage parlor in the local shopping mall, but part of it involves a small Asian woman walking on her back. She returns feeling much better. I am pretty sure if I walked on her back, she would want a bloody goat hide instead.

I can, however, tell you that there is no guy as lucky as me for having a wife who whelps puppies and breathed life into a few that were born by c-section. She cleans any mess a beagle can make, and your imagination can't compete with reality on this. She schedules veterinarian appointments, administers canine medicine (using a spoon to make a peanut butter ball around the pill), and gives the beasts baths when we come home muddy from a hunt. She kills ticks and uses some special power to take care of dog hair that clings to clothes. She feeds dogs, buys dog food when I forget, and takes care of all the grocery store dog treats. I had beagles when we married, and she knew it was not just a hobby but a way of life. She will go to the beagle club with me and has run dogs when I could not. She naps on the couch with those dogs, and that may be the reason she needs the little woman to walk on her back. I will also take her out to dinner in honor of one of the three murdered Christians named Valentine, and I won't even ask her when she will be ready or why she is late. I don't want to remind her of the day we met when she didn't like me at all.

TRAIL CAMERAS

Technology has been changing our lives forever. There was a time, however, when we used the term to mean more than just electronic technology. You know, fire was once a new technology. Rifling in a gun barrel was once new and improved the accuracy of the smooth-bore muskets. Four-wheel drive, in this country, was first developed in 1905 in Brookville, Pennsylvania, just one county away from where I live. The Europeans designed versions of four-wheel drive before the US. That is one of my favorite bits of technology. I own a muzzle loading shotgun, but firing pins are way better than percussion caps or flint for making the gun go boom when rabbit hunting. Goretex and Thinsulate were great technological developments, too, though I still like some older technology—wool.

Technology now means electronics in popular usage. Perhaps nothing has changed hunting more than trail cameras. A good friend of mine had one stolen (by a relative, who else?). How did he know? Well, the thief was captured in the act by another trail camera! When my buddy went to confront the thief (the group of relatives living in a compound of condemned trailers), the result was five guys picking a physical fight with him! Tough to deny you are the thief when you are caught on camera.

That's the thing: some people have lots of cameras. My nephew must have 20 of them. All year long, he checks the pictures in advance of deer season. He watches these deer as the antlers first spurt and then grow in thick velvet over the summer through the magic of remote, motion-activated photography. The bigger the antlers get, the more excited he becomes. It reaches a feverish pitch in late September, before the advent of archery season, when the bucks are then wearing polished headgear. My nephew is then shaking like a kid on Christmas morning, seeing a pile of wrapped presents after consuming cookies and hot chocolate to boost sugar levels. I can always tell when it happens because my telephone will start lighting up and vibrating like a pinball machine. You youngsters can google "pinball machine" and see what once passed for electronic entertainment, before the days when kids sat in their bedrooms and played games against other people who were in their own homes, connected by the internet. We had to go see other people, even to play video games, going to meet each other at the arcade. Pool is another game you can look up. When I was in college, I had a roommate named Buckets (no clue how he got that nickname), and when we went out to the local pool hall, we often ate and drank for free. He was a master pool player, and I am not. I was the bait, as the two of us were partners and would gamble against others. Buckets would throw a few games, and then, when the money was big, as he would get increasingly agitated with each loss, looking like he was losing his mind-raising bets, he would run the table for a $20 wager.

"I am not contributing much here," I said.

"You are the reason they don't kick my ass," he said, "You're doing plenty."

Where did that digression come from? Oh yeah, pinball. My phone goes berserk as image after image is flooded into my phone for several nonstop minutes. There is no point in picking the thing up until it stops because if you are looking at a picture, a new one arrives and scrolls your phone against your will. Each buck has a name based on the antlers' size or configuration. I know their names and can sing them to the Christmas tune for Rudolph. "You know Crabby and Mossy and Shovel and Scoopy. Branchy and Brutus and Monster and Slammer. But do you recall the most famous atypical whitetail of all . . . Rootball, the big horned whitetail, had a really crazy rack, and if you ever saw it, your lips would even smack. None of the other whitetails would even go near his Rootball head . . ."

At any rate, Rootball looks like you bought a 45-foot Christmas tree with the rootball attached, then took the rootball off, unbound it, shook out the dirt, and put it upside down on his head. The reality is that we rarely know where these massive bucks are in daylight. The pictures are all in the middle of the night, long before shooting hours. Sometimes, my nephew does see these behemoths in the rut and will kill one. Often, these guys that come to the area from Pittsburgh and tromp loudly in the woods will get one in rifle season, as one city slicker inadvertently (he thinks he is still hunting) drives one to his fellow city slicker 600 yards away.

Anyway, technology has definitely changed rabbit hunting, too. I was one of the last guys to get a GPS collar for my dogs, and now I can't imagine going back to running without them. You see, guys obsess over the data.

"You should see this," a club member told me in the beagle club parking lot.

"What's that," I said.

"Check this out, my dog has been averaging 12 miles an hour in here, on a cottontail!"

"Umm, you notice that whenever he loses the rabbits, that dog is running the paths with the intensity of a horse under a barrel racer until it finds a new one? He's running rabbits at four or five miles per hour and finding them at 22 miles per hour. He put a hole in the dividing fence; he was moving so fast he didn't see it. It all averages out," I said, realizing instantly that I had burst a bubble like Debbie Downer entering the room. That being said, GPS has been a real game changer. I remember when a hare would go out of hearing range, and no one knew how far away it was or what it was doing. You just went to a dirt road (or, more commonly, an underground gas line that was mowed and maintained on top), waited until the dogs were audible again, and got ready to shoot. You never knew how many loops it made somewhere else before returning.

My wife, Renee, wears a watch that counts her steps, and since New Year's Day, she has had a goal of getting a certain number of steps each day. To assist in that effort, she has been going rabbit hunting with me. I have her stay between the good cover and the paved road. It isn't common for the rabbits (cottontail) to run towards the road, but it is a problem when it does! She walks around out there, making enough noise to scare the rabbit back, and it doesn't disturb my hunt! There is one place, however, where her role is helpful. There is a farm I hunt that has a narrow row of pines that snakes into a valley right under the hardtop road. I have Renee stay out there and it really does make a safety difference. Not every rabbit utilizes that escape route, but some do, often after a few circles fail to elude the dogs.

"I got 5,000 steps," she said one day after the hunt, "Can you get me a Snickers bar when we stop to get gasoline?"

"Sure," I said, "How many calories are in a Snickers, and how many calories are burned in 5,000 steps?"

"Get a small Snickers," she said.

Trail cameras never came into play in my rabbit hunting until recently. A church member lets me hunt his farm, and they have had some people sneaking on the land lately. Perhaps living on venison. My phone buzzed. A photo came through and I was asked if the picture on that farm, from a trail camera, was me. I was almost offended! This guy trespassing was obviously shorter and "stockier" than me! I obviously need to shed a few pounds, but I didn't look like that guy! He was leaning forward and looked pretty "squatchy," as in Sasquatch, with a hunched-over gait. Plus, this guy obviously had a dark brown, almost black beard. Mine is brown, with some tufts of red and more tufts of grey. I began to reply that it was not me and then I looked at the guy, and realized he was wearing an orange wool vest just like mine! It was identical in every way, and it isn't sold around here. Now, I was perplexed and wondering how I could look like that in the woods. Then, it came to me. I haven't worn that vest in quite a long while. I have Renee wear it to be safe from other hunters while she is walking. She wears a pair of my briar bibs, too, which smashes her chest down flat. She wears one of my fleece shirts, which is too big, and balls up in a mass of fabric on her belly under the bibs. The same thing happens with one of my cotton duck shirts—briar protection, worn over the fleece but also under the bibs, adding another ball of fabric. The beard was her hair blowing over her face. It is the most unflattering picture of her.

"That's my wife getting her daily steps," I texted.

"That explains the small boot track," he answered.

Ahh. Technology. I am never surprised, and I presume I am always on a trail camera, no matter what I am doing. I actually have to use technology right now. After seeing the picture that was texted to me, my wife is demanding her own hunting clothes, that are designed for women.

HEMLOCKS & PINES

One of the recent changes in my hunting season over the last few years has been the addition of Christmas Eve to the days when I can hunt. When I was a kid, way back in the 1900s, rabbit season ended after Thanksgiving and did not return until after Christmas. We now can hunt after Turkey Day but before Christmas, from the end of the rifle deer season through Christmas Eve, and then hare season starts the day after Christmas. Christmas Eve hunting, you must understand, was never a holiday tradition in my family. It was Illegal back then. I have to say, it has become a cherished tradition for me.

If you don't know me, I can tell you that I am prone to being absent-minded. I walked around the office, looking for the keys that were in my hand. I never know where a coffee cup might turn up—I am notorious for putting them on high, flat surfaces to keep the dogs from stealing a lick or two. As a pastor, I am always losing my vehicle in hospital parking garages and parking lots. I once rushed from a hunt directly to a hospital to see a church member who had been in a car accident. I was wearing bibs and a wool pullover. When I finished the visit, I wandered the hospital parking garage looking for my truck, going from one floor of the garage to the next. A hospital employee found me trudging in my boots along the sloped floors of the parking decks.

"Can I help you?" He asked.

"I can't find my truck," I scratched my head, "I forgot where I parked."

"Oh," he said, "Okay. We thought you were a homeless guy casing out the place to rob an unlocked car."

"What?"

"You looked like a homeless guy," he pointed at me to make It clear.

"Oh, what does a homeless guy look like?" I asked.

"You here as a patient?" He asked.

"Nah, I was visiting a church member who was rushed here. I didn't find out about his car wreck until recently." I gave him the card that enables clergy to get free parking.

"You have a good day, Sir."

Anyway, the point is that I lost my truck, and I have done it before then and since. If you have ever been to Geisinger Hospital in Danville, Pennsylvania, then you have seen the largest parking lot I have ever seen. They have a shuttle that loops around the expansive lot and then to the hospital entrance. I rode that thing for a half hour to find my car one time. My current Beagle Mobile has a rooftop tent, awning, and a massive rear bumper with storage cabinets. I obviously have all those things to travel with dogs and be comfortable when I go to field trials to hunting trips.

"Why do you have all that stuff on your truck?" I was asked at a field trial.

"So that I can find it in parking lots," I answered, only half joking. I am forgetful. I miss things in the news, and I can be out of touch with pop culture.

My first Christmas Eve hunt was with Andy Purnell, not many years before he died. I had no idea that we were even allowed to hunt that day.

"You got church on Christmas Eve?" Andy asked me on the phone.

"Well," I was sarcastic, "It Is Christmas Eve. What do you think?"

"But that stuff is all at night, right?" He knew the answer to that question. Many don't know this, but Andy was an acolyte in The Episcopal Church as a kid.

"I am free till 7 o'clock," I said, "What's up?"

"Let's rabbit hunt in the morning!" He said.

"We ain't allowed," I replied.

"It has been rabbit hunting season since deer season ended!" I heard him laugh.

"Shut up!" I said.

"I'm telling you the truth," Andy said, "But I can hear you typing to double-check me."

Sure enough, rabbit season had been expanded. "Well, I'll be," I said.

"How do you not know this?" He chuckled.

"Meh, I miss things. My wife gets mad all the time when I do not notice haircuts that she gets."

"I will meet you at eight o'clock," he said, "Let's get breakfast at your place." That meant the restaurant close to my house which has the best home fries in the entire world. They also serve homemade pepper relish, which varies by batch and ranges anywhere from extraordinarily hot to a flavor just cooler than magma. Yum.

"Alright," I said. This meeting place meant that we would hunt close to me and go to one of my spots. Andy had lots of spots, and if I am honest, he showed me more hunting holes than I ever showed him. He carried his .410 pistol, and we walked into some pines. A brush-up against the snow-filled boughs had him emerge from said pines with his beard covered in snow, and he was puffing frantically to keep his pipe lit. To be honest, he looked a bit like Santa Claus, If Santa started jumping around and complaining about snow falling down his back while wearing an orange vest.

"That is cold!" Andy said. The dogs started a rabbit and headed towards the bottom as we laughed at the snow fiasco and listened. The chase was going great, and we could not stop laughing at the sight of Andy trying to keep his pipe lit through the plop of snow.

"What were you doing off the road?" I laughed. Everyone knew Andy wasn't big for getting into the cover—whether it was thick briars or easy walking.

"I was turning my back to the wind and didn't know I was that close to the trees," he said. As soon as he uttered the words, he knew how he left himself wide open to an insult about his proclivity to shoot from dirt roads and start laughing, "Ha ha ha!" he said.

I barely composed myself to talk through the laughing, "You accidentally left the path!" I wheezed, "And then your laugh was almost a Ho Ho Ho! That would have matched your white beard." We walked over to watch the chase.

"That rabbit is gonna cross the spoil pile," I said. A spoil pile is a topographic feature left after an area has been surface mined for coal.

"You still got that sighthound in there to follow footprints in the snow, right?"

"Yeah," I said.

"We will be fine,"

It then occurred to me that I had Christmas cookies in my pocket. Good ones. Church Lady cookies. The kind that are made with club crackers and layers of butter and chocolate and other stuff.

"Say," I cleared my throat, "Do you want some Christmas cookies?" I said to Andy as we stood on a steep bank, watching my dog take the front through the shale and dirt that was covered with a coat of fresh snow, using his eyes to see rabbit tracks.

"Hold this," I handed Andy my shotgun as I rooted into my inner vest pocket to track down the zip-top bag of snacks. "I gotta get Santa his cookies while he watches my dog work and lead his mutts through this coal mine." I snickered.

He laughed as he grabbed my back with a big paw of a hand and kicked my legs out. He eased my weight to the ground and pushed me down the steep bank towards the bottom where the dogs were chasing, "Don't get my cookies wet!" He yelled as I slid about 30 yards down the hill. "HO! HO! HO!" Andy mocked me with a laugh as I rolled over to my stomach, looking uphill at him as I slid away.

It was Christmas Eve, and we were acting like little kids. Did we shoot rabbits? A couple. We shot a couple.

"You bring the coffee?" He asked as we loaded the dogs back into the truck.

"You know I did," I said, grabbing my thermos, "Those cookies make you thirsty?"

"Yup."

"I filled his travel mug 2/3 with coffee. Andy always added about a half cup of that powdered coffee creamer. French vanilla or hazelnut. Maybe more than a half cup, as it obliterated the coffee taste. He carried a container of it in his glovebox! I have hunted on Christmas Eve since then. Some years, we have snow. Some years, we do not. But I always think about my first Christmas Eve hunt with Andy, and then I go home and get ready for candlelight services at church.

My father and I made a ritual of hunting snowshoe hare on the day after Christmas every year. That was opening day for hare here in Pennsylvania, and not many guys knew where to find them back then. I lived in the northern part of the state and could walk to a stand of hemlocks that was full of the white ghosts. We frequently chased them, but the short season meant that we were only able to get a few each year. By the time we could hunt them, I all but had them ready for the hunt, running them for months. When you run the same hare all the time, they get playful and almost don't fear the dogs like a beagle club bunny. I was always so enthusiastic on the first day, and Dad could see the excitement on my face.

"Relax, we will be there soon enough!" He said one year.

"Yeah, but there is this one hare that Is massive; you won't believe it, and I know right where we have to stand to get him!"

And we did just that, and the hare was the biggest I have ever killed, even to this day. And if we managed to get our daily limit of hare (2 per person per day, at that time), then we would relocate to a brushy bottom near a farm and try to get some cottontails, too. It was just what we did on the day after Christmas. We hunted all day with our beagles. It was my favorite day of the year; Dad and I went hunting on the 26th of December like it had religious significance. And while he never ate candy, for some reason, Dad brought peanut brittle to the woods for the start of every hare season. We would eat rock-hard peanut brittle while listening to the hare loop. My life has pretty much gone to the dogs ever since then.

Last year I was hunting Christmas Eve on a piece of land a friend of mine owns. I was putting the finishing touches on my sermon for that night and thinking about Christmas and how Christmas can make us sad when loved ones have gone before us. I thought about those hunts with Dad on the day after Christmas and the hunts with Andy on the day before Christmas, and the way that Christmas is a non-hunting day sandwiched between my new tradition of hunting cottontails on the 24th and my older tradition of chasing hare on the 26th. As the dogs chased that Christmas Eve cottontail last year, I grabbed a hatchet from my truck and cut down a small spruce tree to put in my house. It was small enough to fit in a bucket, covered with a small tree skirt. My wife has been a fan of artificial trees, especially since they invented those pre-lit ones. We had not had a real tree for a few years. I decided that I would put this small spruce on a table in my office.

On that Christmas morning a year ago, I drank my coffee with the odors of that spruce filling the room. It was in the pines where Andy pitched me down the spoil pile on my first Christmas Eve hunt. It was in the hemlocks where Dad and I spent our December 26th hunts. That little spruce seemed to do the trick to conjure both traditions and both evergreen species to the forefront of my memory. While the rest of my family was sleeping, I sat in my office with that tiny tree and had breakfast. Oh, did I tell you that I stopped at the grocery store after cutting that tree down and bought some nasty French vanilla-flavored powdered creamer and a small box of peanut brittle? I poured the flavored powder into my coffee and grabbed a rock-hard piece of brittle. As daylight began to overtake the morning, I forced my nostalgia to stay in the dark as my family began to stir, and we prepared to commence with celebrating the light of the Christ child. Holidays can be tough, but we owe it to our beloved dead to continue with our lives. We must make sure others have cherished memories and traditions, and that is somewhat dependent upon us. We must be joyous and bear the light for others. Merry Christmas, everyone, and keep them running!

In-laws and Outlaws

Well, you know how it goes, there are in-laws, and there are outlaws, and sometimes you are on the "outs" with your in-laws. One of the realities of Thanksgiving in my childhood home was a never-ending barrage of relatives who would stop by to "shake and howdy" with everyone. Okay, everyone had their own meal, but you never knew who might drop in before or after dinner. It started early in the morning when my maternal grandmother would show up to help my mother cook Thanksgiving dinner. When I say help, I mean that she would flit around the kitchen, making passive-aggressive comments to get my mother in a bad mood. "I think you are opening that oven too often, but you do what you want." "Oh, box stuffing? Haven't you been baking enough bread to have some crusty loaves to make your own?" "Store-bought pie crust? That didn't exist when I was raising children." And it would go on like that until the tension in the air got as thick as pea soup—pea soup that was put in the freezer last year.

The real traffic started after dinner when family visitors would randomly show up. Early in the afternoon it was folks stopping for coffee and dessert. Keep in mind that deer season started the Monday after Thanksgiving, and the diaspora relatives would be trickling into town, too. My mother's sister had a husband that came every year. They lived out near Philadelphia somewhere. Uncle Lester was a nice enough guy but wasn't that familiar with the ways of wild critters or the places where they lived. One year, he shot a buck and proceeded to drag it out. It was probably a mile drag or so. People saw him and congratulated him. Several hours later, he was still not seen, and his vehicle (a sedan with tarps in the trunk to catch the blood) was still parked on the hardtop road. Panic ensued about six o'clock, three hours after the deer was killed.

Dad and I had hunted in the morning before Father had to go to work at 3 o'clock, but we had not seen Uncle Lester. They called Dad at work, which never happened. You just didn't call Dad at work. This, of course, was before cell phones, but even at that, it wasn't like the factory had telephones in every hallway. Someone had to find him, and then it was a big production to have someone fill in at his post while he walked to the phone. You only called if it was serious. I once got in trouble at school and was fairly defiant about the matter, feeling I was in the right. I got paddled. Sat down. Then the principal said he was going to call my father at work. I felt the color leave my face, and being right didn't matter anymore. The paddle didn't make me cry; calling Dad at work did!

"We don't know where Lester is!" Mom yelled into the phone. Followed by, "Uh uh. Hmm. Okay. Your father wants to talk to you," Mom handed me the phone, which was attached to the wall of the kitchen.

"Yeah?" I said.

"Have your mother drive you out to Lester's car. Take the big flashlight, all the bulbs for the light, and all the D batteries we have. Take a couple of small flashlights to change batteries in the big flashlight if you need to do that."

"Okay," I said.

"He must be on the main road; they say he shot it back towards the old coal mine. That is close to where we run hare."

"I know where you mean."

"Don't leave that main dirt road. When you get to the coal mine turnoff, you should see drag marks on the snow. If you do not, just turn around and go back to the car with your mother. If you find him, take him out to his care. Tell him I said buck the deer, I will get it get it in the morning. I will be home at 11 o'clock tonight. Don't call me back unless you don't find him or he is dead or something. If he is okay, I will get the details when I get home." Only, he didn't say "buck the deer." Sure enough, I found the drag marks, going the wrong way down the main road. There wasn't much snow, but enough to see a bit of blood. I found Uncle Lester a couple of miles later; he saw my flashlight and came running to me.

"I am right here!" He said. Then, as he neared, "Bobby?"

"Dad sent me, let's get going. You walked the wrong way."

"I gotta get my buck!"

"Dad said buck the deer, he will help you get it in the morning," only I didn't say buck. I wasn't old enough to drive yet, but I had been given permission to use the biggest cuss word, and it felt really rebellious. Everything worked out, and the buck was fine the next day, a little frozen.

Anyway, all these visiting hunters always stopped by on the evening of Thanksgiving to tell hunting stories, drink a beer, and then maybe watch the end of a football game. The house would get claustrophobic with people watching TV in our small living room.

Dad and I always hunted rabbits on Thanksgiving morning. Just to escape the process of my Mom and her Mom getting into each other's way in a small kitchen.

"We ain't in no hurry to shoot a rabbit," Dad would always say. If we could get a good chase until ten o'clock, we would then shoot. Well, he would let me shoot. It can be tough to get a really long chase, and often, the rabbit would hole up after an hour.

"I could have shot that one," my child-self would say, "It was going to hole anyway!"

"Find me a rabbit!" Dad would yell to the dogs and they would leave the hole to beat the brush, "You can shoot later."

The year after "Wrong Way Lester," as the joke came to be called, Dad asked me on Thanksgiving Eve, "How's your patience doing?"

"What?"

"I think tomorrow we will go to a spot that will have a lot more hare than cottontail. You can't shoot a hare until after Christmas. You gonna be able to tell the difference and resist?"

"I think so."

"You better know so."

"I will be careful," I said.

"I am only worried about the first circle if it is a hare; it might short circle and not run very big. Otherwise, it will be obvious by the size of the circles."

An overgrown clearcut adjacent to a huge stand of hemlocks in the Allegheny National Forest was our destination. Tall grasses were feeding the cottontail and hare; the hare would run the hemlocks, and the cottontails would stay closer to the sumac and cattails, running into the thick cover where the treetops were left from the last logging operation. The first rabbit ran into the hemlocks briefly and circled back.

"Shoot it," Dad whispered in my ear as it hurtled across the dirt road toward the thickets. I collected the cottontail before the dogs arrived to tear it up potentially. After 20 minutes or so, I saw a big hare burst out of the cattails and into the hemlocks, crossing the road 80 yards in front of me. A few minutes later, the dogs opened up with a chorus of baying, and off they went. "That was a hare!" I said.

"Good," Dad lit his pipe and walked towards the truck. He unloaded his gun and told me to do the same. We sat on the tailgate and just talked. The kind of talk where there are long bits of silence. We joked about Mom and Gram. Then we would talk about school. When the dogs would come back, we would get up to look for the hare and watch the dogs cross after. This was before GPS, and the two beagles we owned would go way out of hearing, and we had no idea where they were. I am going to guess that they were running for about three hours or so when they started getting close for about the fifth time, and their frantic chase song was getting louder. I am going to guess it was three hours or so, only because we got home right before meal-time, which was one o'clock. Mom had a rule that we needed to be back by then, but we sometimes were late. The chase may have been longer than three hours. Like I said, there was no GPS handheld with a clock on it then.

Dad tapped out his pipe and started sprinting for the hem-locks. He was 6'2'" and long-legged. I am only 6' and long-waisted. Years of smoking took away the four-minute mile that he could rattle off in his youth, but his ¼ mile sprint was still pretty strong, even at almost 60 years of age. The dogs were a little pooped but were not easy to catch; They were not too difficult, however, once he was close enough to yell, "Down!" He grabbed Princess and leashed her. She was the tougher to catch. I was there just a few seconds later and leashed Duke. We cleaned the cot-tontail rabbit and headed for home, about a half hour away. We pulled into the driveway, and I put the rabbit in water to soak in the basement refrigerator, where we kept mostly fishing bait and Dad's Schmidt's beer. Then, we put the dogs in the fenced yard.

"You want me to put them in the kennel or let them run in the yard?" I asked, "I bet they are content enough not to try and dig out?"

"Let's kennel them," he said, "Lord knows who might stop and make them bark or who might accidentally open the gate."

The kennel was an above-ground shed that Dad built, with above-ground runs with wire floors over a cement pad to catch the refuse. He had electricity run to the kennel and even an electric heater he could run. Each wire run extended into the insulated shed, where you had a box with a lid.

"You like Turkey?" He asked.

"Yeah, why?"

He climbed the three steps to get into the shed. I followed and was confronted with odor. Not dog odor (I had to clean that entire kennel every day), but the smell of food.

"What is this?" I asked.

"I started a crockpot of rabbit stew early this morning before daylight. You can eat all the turkey you want, but after we eat dinner, I think we will come out here. We have all kinds of people stopping by to hunt this year. Your Mom's brother is back in the area, and he has a few kids with him. Lester will no doubt be around. There won't be enough seats!" He pointed at two lawn chairs he must have brought to the kennel from the shed. "We can sit out here and eat supper. They will leave faster if I am not there. Plus, I only left five beers in the refrigerator; they won't stay too long!"

After dinner (I went light on the turkey) we chatted and had dessert. It got to be 3 o'clock or so, and Dad said, "Hey, where is the other leash?" Our leashes always hung on a peg just inside the back door/mud room.

"I hung mine up," I said.

"I did, too," Dad said. We always had leather leashes with French snaps. I checked the floor. Nothing.

"Hey!" Dad yelled in the general direction of my Mom, "We're going to run out to where we hunted this morning and look for that leash we lost!"

"Okay!" Mom yelled.

"Hurry back," Gram said, "Lots of company is coming."

"Do my best," Dad said, and we drove out of the driveway, headed in the wrong direction to get where we hunted.

"What's going on?" I asked.

"Here," Dad threw the leash to me, which had been in the truck all along.

"I don't understand . . ." I held the leash.

"If they see my truck, they will find me. I am parking it behind the kennel." He laughed. We rushed around, parked, and closed the truck doors as quietly as possible. He reached into the bed of the truck he pulled out a cooler with four beers and four RC colas. And a big piece of cardboard and tape.

"What's the cardboard for?" I asked.

"Blocking the window in the kennel so that they can't see the light from the kitchen." I rooted into the cooler and got a pop. Dad let the dogs out of the sleeping boxes and into the shed part of the kennel. The beagles were balls of energy, as they were not in that part of the kennel very often.

"I almost forgot!" He slinked out of the kennel, closing the dogs in, and returned with a big smoked ham hock for each of them. Their eyes were bulged in ravenous zeal. We sat with the dogs, talked, and ate rabbit stew on paper plates. We used an old radio to put some music in the room for the times between dialogue when we just scratched a dog's ear. I put it to a station that played older country music on AM radio, the music Dad liked. About 7 o'clock, Dad said, "Go get the dogs their supper. See who is still here and tell them you are feeding dogs and that I am thinking about going out to look for that leash again."

"PHHEW!" I spit RC Cola out at the thought of being gone this long for a leash.

"Hi, Mom," I said.

"That took forever!" Mom answered, "I was worried."

"No one here?"

"My brother was here with his three boys, but they are gone. Your grandmother went to my sister's house. She took Uncle Lester's family with her, except for Lester. He wants to talk to your Dad."

"Okay," I grabbed the bowls of Purina covered in turkey gravy and went out to the kennel.

"All clear?" Dad asked.

"Just Lester, everyone else left."

"Here," he opened the doors of the run to put in the food, and he added a second water bowl for each hound, "Those ham hocks will make them thirsty."

We walked into the house, and Lester was there, "You went out all that time looking for a cheap leash?" Lester laughed his sort of hoarse cackle.

"Shit," Dad said, "If I sent my little boy out into the night air to fetch your bucking ass last year, you know I wasn't going to strand my favorite leash." Only he didn't say bucking. Happy Thanksgiving.

QUIET TIME

The early fall was always a bittersweet time of year for me when I was growing up, way back in the 1900s. Summer, you see, was this wonderful celebration of life wherein we kids got sprung from our incarceration at school. Then, after a few wonderful months, our parole was revoked, and we found ourselves back in the classroom. Granted, as I got older, the summers were less carefree because I was old enough to work. However, this also meant I had more money than what my paper route paid; delivering papers was my first income when I first bought my beagles as a younger kid. Summer jobs meant more dog money.

While the return to school was somewhat sad, it also meant that it was now autumn—glorious, beautiful autumn! Hunting season was the focus of my life, and while I trained beagles all year long, it was in the fall that we were finally allowed to hunt. Today, we can hunt beginning in mid-October, but back then, we had to wait until November. Oh, I still remember waking up with excitement to walk to the high school—I walked a back way, adjacent and through some lands where I would often chase rabbits. Sure, it was technically so close to town that you could not legally hunt there, but you were allowed to chase rabbits, and it had lots of them. Oh, I should mention that back then, we were not allowed to chase rabbits in the summer. We called it "The Quiet Season" because we had no hound music. No one was allowed to train or condition dogs in the summer. The prevailing mindset was that no baby rabbits or game birds would survive if dog training were allowed. The only place you could train dogs was on grounds owned by a club, inside a fenced enclosure, all of which required fees to be paid to the state government. Those then required membership dues at the club. Don't get me wrong, I enjoy beagle clubs, and I belong to two of them today, but there is nothing like a good chase in the wild to get the blood stirring and for the thrill of the chase.

One of the first signs of fall was the annual trip to buy school clothes. Mom would load my sister and me into the car, and we would head off to the shopping mall for the annual excursion. The resulting purchases were designated as "school clothes" and could not be worn anywhere else. My inventory was pretty simple—three pairs of blue jeans, five shirts, and a new pair of sneakers. I am not saying we were poor, but the idea was that all denim jeans look mostly alike. Mom did laundry on Wednesday, so three pairs was plenty for the week. Five shirts meant that I never had to wear the same shirt twice in one week. When winter arrived, I got my wardrobe doubled when more jeans, shirts, and sneakers arrived at Christmas.

At any rate, school clothes were treated as if they were made of paper. Only worn to school and removed as soon as you got home from school. I ran home to let my dogs out of the kennel and into the yard, making sure that I changed all my clothes first. Woe to me if a muddy paw print jumped against a shirt designated for school. I still remember the first day of school smelling like the clothes racks at the store, everyone wearing brand new shirts and pants, and the hallways squeaked with an echo as the new soles of new shoes hustled along the tile floors, looking for classrooms. Walking in the halls on the first day of classes was as loud as a basketball game in terms of rubber soles!

I was one of those kids who would rather be outside, so I rarely brought homework home. Now, don't get me wrong, I still did it, but I would use any available time to get it done before I left to go home. If I turned in a test, and we had the whole class to do it, then I would do homework in other subjects. I would work at lunch even. I used the whole study hall. I guess this got me a reputation for being a nerd, but I was a nerd who spent his time in the hills and on the streams. My non-school clothes all had block patches sewn on the knees and were a couple of inches too short from growth spurts. Every morning, I was walking through the old woodyard that once provided wood for the local mill. They had a new storage location, and the old yard had become a tangle of thickets and brambles. Every morning walk to school, I saw big rabbits everywhere. This was in September, and the quiet season was over. I wanted to chase those rabbits! So, I formed a plan.

Attendance was taken at home room. That formed the official registry of being present or absent. No other teacher did roll call. During the first period, a mimeographed (before photocopies they used this wet ink) sheet was sent to all the teachers, which listed all absences. I just decided that it was possible to disappear when the bell rang for us to leave homeroom and go to the first period. Just act casual, go slow, walk with purpose, and then wait by the stairwell. When everyone was in a classroom, I could walk to the tree line and make my home. Dad would be at work, Mom would be running errands, and I could sneak the beagles out of the kennel and into the briars! Our kennel had an insulated shed with above-ground runs leading out of it. Each run had a sleeping box in the shed. I would just leave my boots and old clothes in the shed, and change before getting the dogs.

Much to my surprise, the plan worked perfectly. I kept waiting for a teacher to say something or notice that I was missing. Part of being a nerd, I guess, means being trusted. I didn't skip every day, and never if I had a test. Oh, the quiet season was over, and the hound music had erupted! Well, I got to thinking, why limit myself to the area between my house and the school? I could walk south from my house with the dogs and find rabbits there, too. Heck, I could even find hare there, which weren't all that common then, let alone now. Whoo! Now I was running the big circles, having the best time I could imagine. Not being satisfied there, I went to the Gordon farm. We often hunted there. By now, it was October, and I could hunt in a month. I may as well do some scouting!

Every week, it seemed, I would get away with this. I was dumbfounded at my luck. I had a great chase at Gordon's that ended up headed along a pine row towards the old Tucker place. It looked like someone had cut all the poplar and birch down. Now, the land wasn't posted (then, it is now), but no one was allowed to cut trees. Someone had made an illegal cut, no doubt for firewood, and there was now goldenrod and early growth that wasn't there before. It was full of rabbits. I was so excited to learn this and couldn't wait to tell Dad. Then, I realized I could not tell Dad. I should be at school. I was walking Duke and Princess back home to get them back in the kennel before Mom and Dad got home and took a shortcut through the lower pasture at Gordon's farm. I heard the snort. Damn. That was the bull, normally in the upper pasture. I released both dogs from their leashes and started sprinting for the fence. The dogs must have sensed the situation since they quickly passed me. I was swinging leashes over my head and picking up speed. Granted, as far as nerds go, I was hardy and tough. But I was never fast. I was that day. I could have outrun the star running back at our school. I saw the fence. Three strands of barbed wire. This wasn't my first go-around with this bull. Sometimes, if the terrain was flat, you could dive over all three strands just from the accumulated adrenaline. On some inclines, you could launch yourself under all three, going close to a fence post. Then, there were days like this one. I was going to have to go between two strands. But they looked closer than usual. I felt the snout. The bull touched me. The horns were close. I angled hard right. A rookie move is to go hard left after that, but if the bull overruns, then you are playing into his game. Right again. Now, I am running away from the fence. As the bull came close again, I made two lefts, putting me back on course for the fence.

I often feel that adrenaline junkies simply had a childhood free of worries and not enough bulls. I can tell you that the Gordon bull made me realize that no one should ever ride one. By this point, I was not only fast but a world-class high jumper. Despite the incline, I dove over all three stands. The dogs were waiting for me. I walked up the hill, and Claude Gordon was laughing.

"I didn't know you were coming," he said, "Or I would have told you where he was pastured! Shouldn't you be in school?"

"Yeah," I said. We laughed. Was Claude going to snitch on me?

I got home, put the dogs away, and realized while changing clothes that I hadn't changed my shirt before running the dogs. I had the slightest scratch on my stomach from the barbed wire— no blood, but a nasty rip in my school shirt. I stewed for the rest of the day. I can't just hide a shirt. There were only five good ones!

After supper, I asked Dad to walk out with me to feed the dogs. He always knew that was a time for father-son talks. Before the dogs were fed, I confessed the whole thing. Then I filled the water bowls.

"How's your grades?" he asked

"What?" I asked, "Why?"

"Sounds like you are skipping school once a week."

"Sometimes less," I said.

"Sometimes more?" he asked.

"Yeah," I looked at my feet.

"Well," he said, "I will make you a deal."

"What?"

"You can only do it once every two weeks, and I won't tell your Mom or the school. As long as your grades stay good."

"Okay," I said.

"And you let me know what day. You can take me to work that day and take the truck to school. But you better pick me up from work at three o'clock."

"But I thought you said I wouldn't be going to school?"

"You ain't too bright for a boy with good marks in school," he laughed, "It is almost hunting season. I will put your gun, gear, and dogs in the truck before your mother wakes up. Just don't get caught."

"What about this shirt?" I asked.

"No problem," he tore it in half, popped the hood on the truck, and checked the oil with it."

"What are you doing?" I whispered as loud as I could.

"Follow me," he winked as we walked into the house. "Hey, Paula!" he yelled.

"What?" Mom walked into the kitchen.

"I reached in the hamper. I needed an old rag to check the oil and thought this was my shirt; I ruined it."

"Well, what is he going to wear now?" she sighed a complaint.

"No one cares what a nerd like him wears," he winked, "Let him wear a damn long-sleeved cotton duck briar shirt for all I care!"

On the first arranged covert sneak day, I drove Dad to work.

"Did you know someone cut a bunch of wood behind Tucker's?" I asked.

"Probably Tucker," Dad said.

"It is full of rabbits," I said.

"Your grades fall, and this thing is over," Dad said.

"Why are you doing this?" I asked.

"A boy ought to have all the responsibility he can take and all the fun he can handle. Just take care of your marks at school."

"Thanks," I said.

"Oh," Dad said, standing on the road with the door open, "I told Claude about this. Ask him where the bull is," he grinned.

"Okay," I said.

"Your Mom is okay with me buying you a new shirt," Dad said, "Stay safe. I can't check the oil with your hide!"

If you knew my Dad, then you would know that those words meant way more than saying "I love you" does in most homes.

Morning Dew

I am seeing a little color in the trees, and hunting season is just around the corner. The summer has been dry, and in my experience, that is good for cottontails. Naturally, dry weather isn't as optimal for hare. Wet springs and summers can be bad for cottontails, which have their young right on the ground, sometimes in the open. In lowlands, an all-day rain can fill the small depression where newborn rabbits are nested with hair that the mother pulls out of her coat. It is no secret that I am not thrilled about cutting grass, and in my neck of the woods, July and August were months of very infrequent mowing. I have neighbors who roll their lawns, aerate them, add fertilizer, plant expensive grass seed, and even irrigate their yards. Me? I mow it when it is wet, letting the clumps smother future growth. As a result, my lawn is populated by the hardiest of plants—weeds. Oh, I have Queen Anne's Lace, stinging nettles, and even burdock. I know people who sow expensive grass seed; my dogs drop burdock in the yard that they collect while hunting. When it gets as dry as we were over the late summer, then I have the only green lawn in town. We were under a drought warning, and watering lawns was strictly forbidden. My green lawn looks great from the road, where you pass it at 35 mph and do not realize that it is a well-groomed lot of weeds with a little grass and clover mixed in.

Lately, since the beginning of this month, the arrival of meteorological autumn, the grass has greened up, and my bumper crop of crabgrass and buckhorn plantain has gone nuts, and I am busy in the field with the dogs. The weather has cooled, and we have experienced the return of morning dew. I love morning dew, and it can make an average dog look great! Lately, I have been getting some screaming fast chases on morning dew in a big sorghum field on a farm. The rabbits are found in the nearby thickets, and then they burst into the sorghum and proceed to run circles that are shaped more like mazes and Hebrew letters. I was listening to the hounds run a big cottontail in the shape of a series of adjacent lameds; the Hebrew name for the letter that makes the sound of an L. Lamed is the last letter in ketal, the Hebrew word for dew. I started thinking of Psalm 133:3: "It is like the dew of Hermon, which falls on the mountains of Zion. For there, the Lord ordered his blessing, life forevermore." Zion was a small hill in comparison to Mount Hermon, which is over 9,000 feet in elevation and is often snow-covered. Meltwater forms the beginnings of The Jordan River. The verse reflects an idea that dew, often the only moisture in ancient Israel, must have dropped off the mountain under cover of darkness and then covered the land with life-giving water. This is how they explained how water shows up without rain. Today, we talk about thermodynamics and the formation of water droplets through condensation, but I think the psalm is much more poetic.

Lamed is the tallest letter in the Hebrew Alphabet and is shaped like a shepherd's staff, and the word lamed means to goad, like using a staff to move livestock. I watched this rabbit zigzagging in overlapping lameds, running through dew-drenched sorghum, and the dogs were absolutely locked on to the scent as the wet crop held the scent, allowing the hounds to run with their heads held high. Oh, don't get me wrong, I enjoy watching good hound work when dogs are able to solve tricks that the rabbit makes to fool the hounds and cease the chase in tough scenting conditions. I appreciate a big-nosed dog solving olfactory riddles and sorting through the labyrinthine changes that a rabbit will make in order to optimize its chances of eluding pursuers by seeking dirt, gravel, rocks, and bare ground in the driest of conditions. I really do like those chases, but I like a good driving chase even better, at least for the music! This particular rabbit made his way to the end of the field and burst into the goldenrod of an adjacent property (did I mention I have some of that goldenrod in my yard, too?) and that resulted in big circles that looked more like rounded squares.

There is just something magical about dew. I can't say enough about it when it comes to making things right! Oh, and after those dogs have been chasing in the heat for months, this dew makes it look like their noses are attached to the rabbit by an invisible string, and almost all of the chases will be long until the rabbit decides that it is in his best interest to take this endeavor to the subterranean realm and hide out until the dogs have left. That can even be risky; I have a small dog that can get in there pretty far—too far for my liking.

"Where are my boots?" I asked my wife, Renee, one night?"

"You are kidding, right?" She asked.

"No."

"Oh, okay," she sighed and moved her hands to her hips. That is never a good sign. "Well, you have a pair on the floor in the middle of the kitchen, another in the bathroom next to the tub, and there's a pair in the trunk of my car; I do not know why, there are three pairs in the closet where all the others should be, and there are two pairs beside the hamper."

"There's a pair in your car?" I asked.

"Yes."

"Are they my rubber boots?"

"Yes," she said.

"I wonder how those got in there?" I asked.

"Well, a few months ago, you took my car to run dogs a few mornings when you were driving someplace far away. You were scouting for rabbits at a place you drove by after leaving a cemetery for a funeral. Or something like that."

"Oh yeah," I said, "That was back when we had dew, before the heat wave! Are they in the car, where?"

"Follow your nose," she said.

"I am not a beagle," I replied.

"You don't have to be. That's a stink that no one can go 'nose blind' to. I was driving somewhere and had to stop and move them to the trunk to avoid the stench. I ordered groceries for pick up at the grocery store; the poor kid almost fell over when he put the groceries in there." Covid has ushered in drive-through grocery pick-up at the local market.

"Really?" I asked.

"I told you to get them out of there and that I wasn't going to touch them! That was four days ago."

"I don't remember that," I scratched my chin.

"Probably because you were too busy fussing with your tracking collars."

"Oh yeah, I had to get some crud out of the area where the collar slides into the transmitter. I need to get those boots. The dew has returned, and my other boots are waterproof, but the moisture is hard on the leather.

"Good," Renee said, "And while you are at it, get those boots by the hamper put away too."

"I don't know where the hamper is," I said.

"I guess that explains the blob of dirty clothes I keep finding in the bathroom closet," Renee said, "Just get the boots out of the bedroom."

"Okay," I said.

I have been sloshing in dew ever since. The only thing better is frost. Oh, I love a good frost, which is frozen dew. When it begins to thaw and steam, the cool air makes for a high scent and lots of great chases, with no need to worry about the dogs getting too warm. I better get those insulated boots ready, too, thinking of frost. I will wait a few days before I ask Renee where I put them. My rubber boots had a pair of wet socks in them, which happened when I took off my boots to drive and then stepped out of her car before putting my shoes on. I just threw those socks into the boots and then put my shoes on. Whew, a few months in the trunk really ripened them up. No matter, autumn is here. Some see it as the harbinger of winter, but I see fall as the last climactic rush of summer. Beautiful foliage, hunting of all kinds, lower temperatures, and that good old dew that coats the ground here in the Appalachian Mountains. Dew is a blessing, as the psalms say, and hunting season is just around the corner.

Ashes to Ashes, Stardust to Stardust

They say any element heavier than Hydrogen was made in a star. Hydrogen fuses into Helium. And that fuses to form heavier elements. The heavier stuff will be found towards the center of a star, like metals. Gold, Silver, platinum, and the less precious stuff are forged in the cosmic furnaces. When a star dies, the elements are scattered. Our planet is made with the remains of dead stars. People are fond of pointing out that we are made of stardust. I was thinking about that this week. I have been avoiding the beagle club with COVID-19 and letting the old timers have the club running grounds. I am constantly officiating funerals with lots of people being exposed to me; the last thing I want to do is give a virus to an older member. So, I have been running in the wild. Everyone who has hunted with Andy Purnell will tell you that they know his secret spots, but I actually do know them. I have been in those spots a lot, the safe ones—some are prone to rattlesnakes before winter.

Andy and I would run dogs and chat. In some spots we would just train dogs, no hunting, just to make sure that no one else found them by following us in hunting season. Sometimes, we would run a place so much that we would know the habits of particular rabbits, the same as when you get a bunny in a beagle club that tends to run the same pattern every time you find it.

"That rabbit is familiar," I said, listening to the dogs one day in November.

"The third circle will cross the fork of the dirt road, running over that flat rock," Andy said.

"Yep."

"We shouldn't shoot it until the third circle," Andy said.

"You want to get it?" I asked.

"Why?" he shrugged.

"I know you like staying on the paths."

"For a guy that gets in the brush as much as you," Andy puffed on his pipe, "You should be a judge."

"I ain't a fast enough runner," I said.

"Fast enough," he smiled.

"I don't know enough about dogs to evaluate them," I protested.

"I won't disagree with you there," he laughed.

"Go stand at the Y in the road," I said, walking away.

"Where you going?" he yelled.

"Don't you worry," I said and headed for a patch of greenbrier. I heard Andy laughing. He knew I was headed to a spot where the rabbit would go on the fourth circle.

BOOM! I heard Andy's .410 pistol bark. "Son of a b—-" Andy yelled. He had missed! The rabbit ran right to me. I dropped it with one shot from my double barrel.

"Well," Andy yelled, "You only shot once, so you must have got it."

"I always get it," I said, "I get at the edge of the brush. They are moving slower."

"They are only slower in front of your dogs!" he yelled back, "Mine are here too! You must have gotten lucky!"

We ran another rabbit, guns unloaded, sitting on a log until it was time for him to go to work at Lion Country Supply and for me to do hospital visits. That was a few months before Andy died from cardiac failure. I was at that Y in the road recently, running a rabbit that runs remarkably similar to the one I shot that day years ago. I won't shoot him this fall if he makes it that long. I was thinking about stardust as the rabbit passed me. Why?

When Andy died, the town where the funeral was held was jammed full of pickup trucks with dog boxes in the bed. They lined the streets like a parade was going to start. The funeral was standing room only as I walked in an hour before the service started.

"Can I get his wedding ring?" Andy's widow, Lisa, asked me. Andy had been cremated.

"I will get it," I said and walked to the funeral director and asked him.

"What ring?" the funeral director asked.

"His wedding band," I said. He looked nervous. The funeral director who worked for him walked towards the back, closing the door behind her. I walked back to the urn with the ashes, where Lisa was greeting people. "They are getting it," I said. A few minutes later, the guy approached.

"They didn't give us the ring," He said, "The State Police probably have it." That sounded odd to me. I pushed the idea aside, getting ready to officiate the service. It was going to be tough to do without getting emotional. When I am at a funeral for someone close to me, I keep a memory of a time when the deceased made me angry, ready to think about if I get too sad to keep speaking. I pause, and the memory pops into my head to help me settle. If that doesn't work, I bite the inside of my cheek. I bit my cheek hard to get through that funeral.

The next day, I called a state trooper I know and asked why the police would have the wedding band. He told me that would not happen. I told Lisa to call the coroner. She got a copy of the coroner's report, and it said that the ring was taped to Andy's hand, and the clothes he was wearing were there, too, with the body. I thought the guy might have stolen the ring, an odd thing.

Lisa called my cell phone, "Hello," I answered.

"I scheduled a meeting with that funeral director," she said.

"Good idea," I said.

"Will you take me?"

"Yeah," I said, "Sure."

"Good," she said, "I am afraid that I will get mad. You need to keep me calm."

"No problem," I said.

I know a lot of pastors and funeral directors. I did some calling. I am told that the guy was previously in legal trouble that got him in enough trouble that he can own a funeral home but he has another worker doing the work. I was also told that he once beat his wife on Main Street. I can't prove that these things are true, and I didn't try to confirm them. But his peers and my colleagues said it was the case.

It was cold and snowy when we met him. Tiny, powdery snowflakes that he was shoveling as we arrived. A broom would work better. Into the office, we went. He sat behind his desk, and Lisa and I sat on the opposite side.

"Did you find the ring?" Lisa asked.

"It never arrived here," he leaned back in his chair like we were discussing a ball game or pizza.

"It had to," I said.

He dialed a number, his desk phone on speaker mode. One ring and an answer "Hello?"

"Yes," the guy put a foot on his desk, "I am here with the Purnell family." He didn't recognize me as the officiating pastor a week earlier. He thought I was a relative.

"Oh yeah," the guy on the other end said.

"Yes," he slouched in his office chair, "You told me that there was no ring on the body when you did the cremation, right?"

"That is correct," the voice asserted.

"Okay," he put both feet back on the desk, "Goodbye."

"What does that prove?" Lisa asked.

"The ring never made it here," he said.

"We contacted the coroner," I said, "You're a liar." I was wondering what pawn shops I had to seek to get the ring back.

"You can't talk to me like that!" he stood and was shouting. Lisa began to cry.

I stood. And in a very calm voice, I said, "You better calm down. Because if you plan on going in this direction, I will give you a hell of a lot more trouble on Main Street than your wife did." I shoved his desk towards him. He sat down and rolled his chair backward. His eyes were like silver dollars. Yeah, I can't believe I said that either. The woman who works for him pulled us aside.

She handed me the ring and told Lisa that she should not pay a bill if she received one. It will be free. She apologized and said she went back and found the ring. It went through the cremation process. It only survived the heat because it was made of titanium. All the precious gold had boiled out of it, and the once shiny titanium was now charred and blackened. That was the second time I held that wedding band. The first time was at their wedding when I held them both high with the wedding liturgy that says, "These rings are the outward and visible sign of an inward and spiritual grace . . ." Now, I held the ring again. We walked outside. No one checked for the ring. They burned it. I was shocked.

"That was some gangster shit, Ford," Lisa said as we left the funeral home.

"What?" I asked.

"You just threatened to kick a guy's ass on Main Street."

"Sorry about that," I saw her watery eyes. I am not touchy-feely, but I reached down and held her hand, making sure that the wedding band was between our palms."

"I didn't expect that from a pastor," she said.

"I hear that from time to time," I said, pressing the ring into her hand so she grasped it as we neared my truck.

"You were supposed to keep me from getting mad!" she said.

Months later, Mike Leaman, Cody Mathis, and I held a small ceremony in one of Andy's favorite hunting spots. We put his ashes, as requested by Lisa, where we had just hunted and shot some hare. It just occurred to me recently that the gold, forged in the blast furnace of a star and boiled out of the wedding band by a crematorium, must have been mixed into those ashes in tiny flakes. "Ashes to ashes and dust to dust," as the liturgy says. Stardust.

Rain Man

The month of July has been brutally hot here in Pennsylvania. More than that, we have now reached almost five months of my wife, Renee, working from home, due to her office at the university being closed to the coronavirus. She is online all day, and she tends not to like certain disturbances. What kind of disturbances? Well, for one, barking beagles.

"Yes," Renee says in her work voice to a gaggle of coworkers crammed into a Zoom meeting, "I think we can install that module to the curriculum without too much diffi—"

"Baroo! Howl! AWWWW!" the beagles interrupt her as they notice someone walking their dog past our house. The dogs take turns, like sentinels on the wall at Guantanamo, perched on the back of the couch with their heads under the window blinds. When an on-duty beagle notices any violators—dog walkers, joggers, bicyclists, mailman, UPS, FedEx, neighbor coming home, neighbor leaving, squirrel (high alert) rabbit (red hot alert) bird, or a leaf blowing in the wind—he or she will then, as the on-duty sentry, sound the alarm. It takes about point-two seconds for the rest of the pack to start barking as well. This has happened so much in this hot weather that my wife can react in point-three seconds. She mutes her Zoom meeting, then yells, not in her pleasant work voice, but in her marital voice, "Will you shut those blanking beagles up!? I am in a meeting!"

That is when I spring into action to get them calmed and quiet. I yell at them or distribute the dust. What dust? Well, I pulverize milk bones now. This is what I have been reduced to doing with my wife at home all day in meetings that need quiet, and me being stuck at home working from the phone. It is bad enough that she has to put a fake background behind her so that no one sees the random beagle bouncing through the background. I like the miniature Milk Bones, but they are in short supply, as well as everything else. The massive Milk Bones, made for giant dogs, are always around and seemingly always on sale somewhere. I put a bunch of them on a towel, cover them with another towel, and pulverize them into near dust with a hammer. This, as you can imagine, makes a bit of noise, so it has to happen at night, after the meetings. Once pulverized with a hammer, I smash them further with an old wood dowel, rolling it over them. The dust goes into a plastic container.

When my lowly mutts shut down online higher learning, I spread a palm full of dust on the kitchen floor. It takes them a while to find it all, and they normally forget what they were barking at. A new duo of sentries takes a watch. This happens several times per day. The real problem has been the high heat and the fact that it has been in the 90s during the day and only cools off to 70 or so by dawn. Oh, and the bulk of my job, hospital and nursing home visits, has been canceled. I have a Regal dog box with fantastic insulation against heat and cold, and I would typically load those dogs up in the morning, run them for a few hours, and then go to work. They stay cool in the dog box, traveling from one hospital to the next during the workday. Not in this high heat and humidity.

"Are they worse than usual?" Renee asked.

"Oh yeah," I answered, "Way worse."

"Can't you do something?" Renee switched from her marital voice to her work voice.

"They need some time on rabbits," I said, "It has been over a week."

"What do you do about that?" she asked

"You won't believe me."

"Why?" she asked, "Is it illegal?"

"No," I said, "Just weird."

"What is it?"

I grabbed my phone and opened one of my weather apps. I have a few of them. "See this," I said, pointing at a blob of red in Ohio.

"Yeah," she said, "You driving to Ohio?"

"No," I said, "But Ohio might come here."

"What?"

"I may not use computers as much as you, but I have a few things that I have figured out."

"Forecasting the weather?"

"Nope," I said, "But close. You know those guys that drive vans into storms, looking for the tornadoes?"

"Yeah," she looked at me.

"Well, when I see the rain coming, I try to get there about a half hour before the rain starts, and the rainfall will keep the dogs cooled down. Depending on the rain, I can get a pretty long run."

"How long have you been doing this?" she asked me.

"Years."

"Is it dangerous?"

"Nah, if it rains too hard, I sit in the truck."

"It works?"

"When it rains, which it hasn't done lately. One day last year, I ran dogs in the morning at Beechton Beagle Club before it got hot. Did visits at the nearby Dubois Hospital, then went to Mountain Laurel nursing home. After that, I had to go to Williamsport Hospital. When I left the hospital, I saw the rain coming and got the dogs dropped at West Branch Beagle Club before the storm started; they got another good chase. Two clubs in one day. That's rare."

"I am impressed," my wife said, "Here, I thought you were not good with technology."

"I ain't very good, but I can see where rain is going," I said.

"Oh Yeah?"

"You don't have to be a weatherman to know which way the wind blows."

"Who said that?"

"Dylan. But it is true." The Ohio rain never made it this far.

A day later, I heard the work voice coming from the kitchen. I mean, home office. "Get in here, please!" I have to admit, I was perplexed. Yeah, we had two squirrels and a UPS lady already, but at the moment, the beagles were sedated, most of them sprawling themselves on the cold linoleum in the home office.

"Now what?" I said.

"Look at this radar!"

"Let me see," I said.

"What do you think?" she said, her bottom lip quivering as she looked at the dogs, fearing they would erupt again.

"Are you in a meeting?" I asked.

"I am logged in," she stared at the radar, "I don't have to talk; I can hear them with my earbuds. My wife has these massive, ugly earbuds. They look like some of her earrings, so I often don't realize they are earbuds with her hair down.

"You know that spot where I went hunting when the guys from Outdoor Life came to town?" I asked her.

"I think I can get there before the rain if I leave right now."

"Here are your tracking collars; I took them off the charger and put them into the duffel bag. Don't hurry home."

"I guess I am a storm chaser," I said.

"More like Rain Man," the marital voice was back.

Third Trick with the Hare

Running in the wild was a great joy for me as a kid. This was because in my adolescent years before I could drive, it was very easy for me to walk a couple hundred yards and be in an area that held bunnies. This was an especially great thing in the summer when I wanted to train dogs and listen to the hound music. It was in July, perhaps, that we could return to the wild if we so desired. Naturally, some beaglers preferred to run inside the fence all year. The irony of that peculiarity was that most of the guys who wanted to run inside the fence all year had very slow dogs that could never go missing. Perhaps the concern was also related to the fact that these were guys who found rabbits for their dogs. Even today, I see gundog brace trials where the shaggers (guys with sticks to shag rabbits out of the brush) are as important as the dogs, and the judges sometimes have to stop walking so as not to pass the beagles. I know people who never hunt with their field trial dogs, preferring to keep them in an enclosure.

Anyway, late summer is a hot time of year, and it makes it difficult for the dogs. Night running was more common then, as the coyotes did not own the woods after dark like they now do. Incidentally, the Pennsylvania Game Commission printed a study in the book of laws that accompanies your purchase of a hunting license a few years ago detailing that the eastern coyote is larger and stronger than the western coyote and, therefore, eats a larger percentage of deer. The reason for this increased size is that the eastern coyote is a result of migration, wherein the western coyote arrived here via the Great Lakes region and interbred with wolves. Our yotes have a sizeable percentage of wolf DNA.

When I was a teenager, our biggest night-time worries were skunks and porcupines. My father would let me stay out all night long in the woods and only imposed a summertime curfew if I went into town. I knew that if I violated this trust, I would be in big trouble and may not be allowed to go out in the woods for a long time.

"Dad," I said one morning after he had his coffee, "Can I take the dogs out tonight to run them." I never asked him anything before coffee.

"Why?"

"Because it's hot now," I held out a thumb, "And we can run in the wild again," I held out my index finger to count my second strong point.

"How are you going to get to wherever you plan to do this? I am working second trick today," he scratched his stubble. Trick, in this case, was interchangeable for shift.

"I am going to walk," I said. I could tell he knew my intentions right away.

"You plan on running a hare?" he grinned. It was a facial expression that combined an appreciation for my plan with a heavy dose of skepticism.

"Yep," I said, "They won't go in a hole. And they go in huge circles. The dogs will fly!"

"You better get there before dark," he sighed, "Because those hemlocks have as many deer as they do snowshoes. You will want to know what you are chasing before the sun sets."

Training collars and GPS were not even close to being used in the beagling world then. We used compasses to get around in the big woods, and it wasn't uncommon to come out of the hemlocks onto a dirt logging road where you had to walk for a mile or so until you saw a landmark that helped you determine where you were. Getting lost could easily happen. I had an old coon hunting light that I planned on using, but the helmet barely adjusted small enough to fit me. An old lensatic compass was my guide into the timber.

Modern hunting is different. For instance, last fall I was catching dogs at dark in Maine, a place where getting lost is a much more serious issue. I had to work very hard to trust my handheld GPS. It was telling me that my truck was parked 90 degrees off from where I felt it was positioned. Oh, it was a half mile away, too. For reasons that I cannot explain, I trust a compass more than the communication between my handheld and the satellites. I had to resist the urge to trust my instincts rather than my technology; I got my compass out and confirmed that the blasted machine was right. Of course, it was correct, and it even compensated for the angle of declination that demarcated the difference between true north and magnetic north. So, off through the cedars I went, struggling to keep the leashed dogs from getting entangled in the ubiquitous, identical cedar trees, each ten inches in diameter. This was the forest that replaced the last clearcut—the perfect habitat for hare.

I digressed. Let's go back to Pennsylvania in the 1980s. I was using a compass and a second-hand coon lamp with a battery that was attached to my belt or should have. The battery may as well have been from a Buick it was so heavy. An older gentleman who retired from hunting gave it to me. I cut his grass every week, and I saw the relic in his garage.

"Jay," I asked, "Can I buy that light?"

"I thought you had beagles," he poked the light with his cane.

"I do, but that could be handy," I said.

"If you can pick it up, you can have it."

It was heavy, and I wondered if many other kids had attempted to lift it but failed like so many who tried to pull Excalibur from the stone in the King Arthur stories. "I got it," I moaned, pretending that it wasn't too heavy. "Thanks."

"You better get some suspenders for that thing. Take this adapter I made to charge it." Jay worked for Ford Motor Company in Buffalo before retiring and returning to Pennsylvania. He could build and design all sorts of things.

Suspenders were no help, as the battery was pulling my britches to the ground. I used a backpack to throw the battery into, and I am still not entirely certain that he did not build that battery as a backup means of powering his whole house. The charge seemed to last forever. The only drawback was that I had to carry a lot of water to stay hydrated from lugging the massive thing up and down the hills of the Alleghenies.

I can't describe to you how wonderful the chases were. Those two beagles thundered through the hills, and the only time I had trouble was if they got onto a cottontail that ran close to houses. People tended not to like the barking at midnight. At least three nights each week I would do this. I came through the door one morning at 7:15 or so, just as Dad was coming home from work. He was working the third "trick" that week. We had a little breakfast together and chatted about our night.

"I was busy," Dad said, "We were a man short, and we had to hustle."

"Dogs crossed the creek," I said, "I got soaked crossing it. Real soft bottom, I sunk knee deep."

"You sure it wasn't the weight from that contraption on your back? I think that battery is tearing the seams of your backpack."

"You might be right," I said.

"The seams on your pant legs are not doing well either."

"Yeah," I poured some juice into a glass, "My legs are a lot bigger from that backpack battery." My mother shook her head as to indicate that sanity was sorely lacking.

I look back at all of this, and I am amazed that I was allowed in the woods, alone, all night long at the age of 15. I was instructed to avoid people if I saw them, which I never did see. Then it happened. My light burned out. Of course, it was the bulb. The battery could probably have powered a small village for a week. I felt my feet wanting to run north and get back home. But I remembered what I was told weeks before when this hare chasing began. If you run out of light, build a fire and sit still until the sun comes up. I caught the dogs in the dark—not easy, as all I had was a small flashlight in my backpack. I tied the leashes to trees and built a fire. I won't lie; I was a little scared, and for some reason, I would have felt safer if I was walking rather than standing still and sitting by the fire. Tiny critters in the brush sounded like monstrous bears, and screeching owls made me think panthers were surrounding me.

Catching the dogs in the dark was a disorienting process, and as the pre-dawn sky brightened, I realized I was closer to my cousin Ray's house than I was to my own. I trod up to his house and sat on the porch until the kitchen light came on. Then I went inside for breakfast and called home.

"Yeah," Dad answered.

"Light burned out. I am at Ray's house. Can you come get me?"

"I'll take you!" Ray yelled.

"Never mind, I got a ride," I said.

"Okay. See you later," Dad hung up.

Back here in the present, I hear coyotes all the time now, and if I am running dogs after dark it is accidental. That was one glorious summer of running, and the cooler temperatures after dark were fantastic for conditioning the dogs. The following rabbit season was the best I had ever experienced to that point in my life. I never did have another great summer of chasing hare at night with such regularity. I was 16 years old the next summer and hanging out with girls seemed to make more sense. I am still thankful for a father who let me roam those hills. Happy Father's Day.

ZOOM

Sometimes, I fear I am becoming my father. Now, I know what you think that means—that I do stuff like yell about the lights being on, get upset if people are wasting leftovers, or fill my gas tank when it gets down to half empty (It is not half full). Oh, I do all those things. Hey, I even tell my family that they do not have to turn the water off so abruptly, causing water hammer in the plumbing system, just like my Dad would complain. No, I am talking about a much different way that I am becoming like Dad. I just realized it recently. Well, in the last couple of months.

I realized that social distancing has not been a hardship for me, at least in terms of my personal life. When I was a kid, I used to say that my father didn't seem to have friends, at least not ones that he "hung out" with on a regular basis. "He is either at work or he is with his family," I said.

"Everyone has a best friend," my buddy said.

"I don't think he does. And the friends he has are just guys from the beagle club."

"No one pops by the house?"

"Yeah," I said, "But only if they need something. Other than relatives. Now that I think about it, the relatives often only stop when they need something too."

"Okay, well, he must get phone calls. Whoever calls him the most often is his best friend,"

"You are probably right," I chuckled.

"What is so funny?"

"Overtime. His most frequent call is overtime from the factory."

All these years later, I think that I am in the same boat. I do not miss restaurants. Even before all this coronavirus stuff, I usually packed a lunch. I never know what my day will bring in terms of hospital visits. I save money with a lunch bucket and eat in my truck. A thermos of soup in cold weather or a sandwich in a cooler during the warmer months is my standard choice. I never really went to stores that much anyway; that has always been my wife's forte. My Dad never signed his paycheck or deposited it once; my Mom always did that. I may deposit my checks, but I do that with my phone now. Sometimes, I will give my debit card to my wife, Renee, when she goes to the store, but she makes more dough at the university than I make! She does have trouble not being around people. Renee is working from home, and I hear some of it.

"I am tired of hearing you talk about Zoom and all the other web pages you can go to for online meetings," I said to her as she closed her laptop, ending a meeting."

"They are platforms, not pages," she looked over her glasses in that bossy sort of way.

"Whatever," I said, "But every conversation you have with every co-worker is the same."

"They are colleagues."

"Okay."

"Do you even know what I do at the university?" she pushed her glasses up and looked through the lenses, trying to bait me into an answer.

"Not really," I said. And I don't, other than it is all online, and that is true even when she is in the office and her "colleagues" are all meeting in the same physical place.

My work has been altered—I can not do hospital or nursing home visits. Heck, I can't do any visits. I have substituted phone calls in place of driving to hospitals. Stupid virus. It goes pretty well, though; as you can imagine, it is tough on people who are older and suffering from hearing loss. Hah, my hearing isn't the best anymore either, so some pastoral care calls are just me and an older guy yelling at each other on the phone. But a couple weeks into this whole mess, I realized that I have to be at church on Sunday mornings for our livestream church service, but otherwise, I could be anywhere during the week, so long as I could make cell phone calls to patients and tend to work stuff from afar. Also, I could wear anything! I ain't talking about pajamas; I mean bibs and brush pants.

Social distancing? How could I possibly avoid people any more than if I went into the woods and just stayed there? I can just run some dogs, have some cookouts, and give my wife a break from the barking house dogs while she is having her online meetings. I will go afield for a couple of days at a time, and as long as I can get a cell phone signal at the top of a hill, I am able to stay there. I take the dogs and might run them as a pack one day and take turns soloing them the next. It makes for a good time alone to think and work on a weekly homily and provides a great place to work on any writing that I have to complete. Over the years, I have been staying in the field with hounds more and more, but in recent weeks, I have really been training hounds. I thought I would share some things that make staying afield with dogs enjoyable rather than uncomfortable.

Rooftop tents are commonly found with an internet search. They vary in style and price. I like a fiberglass top, which is why I have a Maggiolina. You can mount it to the rooftop of a car or SUV. With my pickup, which has a dog box in the bed, I use a ladder rack. I like the fiberglass top because I have never gotten wet, no matter how hard it has rained upon me. The tent bolts on the ladder rack, and I can drive anywhere with it—80 mph on the interstate or an off-road crawl (it is only 130 pounds) into hunting spots. In one minute, the tent can be raised, a ladder extended, and I can climb in and sleep on the mattress that is built into the tent itself. The tent has paid for itself with the money it has saved me by not sleeping in hotels while on long road trips. In fact, I sleep in this tent so much that it feels like home, and I now get to field trials the night before rather than waking up in the middle of the night to drive.

Comfort goes beyond the tent. In all those cowboy movies, the guys sleep on the ground, using a saddle for a pillow and just a blanket. Then, they wake up and move cattle all day. Even when I am training dogs for a few days, I seldom let them run rabbits the entire day, but rather, a few hours in the morning and a few hours in the evening are more typical. What about the rest of the day? It is good to have a comfy chair, some shade, and a place to sit and work in the rain. They sell all kinds of awnings for your 4x4. I have a Foxwing that provides lots of shade for sitting under and also a place for the dogs to cool down. It takes a few more minutes to deploy than the tent, but not much more. It can be attached to a roof rack or any other customized option, as I did for mine. It can handle highway speeds when not deployed.

My tent is comfortable, don't get me wrong. However, my best sleep of the day comes after I put some miles on the dogs at dawn, eat a late breakfast, and then take a nap before afternoon work, phone calls, and writing. I own a camping hammock. You can't find a more comfortable "chair" if you try. When I do camp remotely, I no longer carry a tent. I use my hammock and use a tarp. No need to worry about roots or rocks. Just find two trees and set it up. Shoot, If I am camping from the truck, I can often get by with one tree and attach the other side to my truck's ladder rack.

I kept my eye on a product, waiting for a good deal because it isn't typically cheap. It is a tent that zips right onto the awning, called an Oztent. Why did I want it? It is perfect for two things—a screenhouse on those evenings when the mosquitoes (big enough to outdo any murder hornet in an aerial dogfight) are biting and a dry place in a driving, windy rain that would typically be catastrophic on my awning. The tent anchors the awning fast to the ground in higher winds. I like to run dogs until dark and return to camp. I can either rest in my hammock or sit in a folding chair in the ground tent. Weather is usually the determining factor.

Storage is vital. I have a bumper with swingout storage boxes that lets me pack a lot of gear. I can fit a lot of clothing and a pillow in compression sacks. I also use the storage boxes for tie-out stakes, water bowls, and flashlights—I hate searching for all these necessities. A hammer, tin shears, and a hatchet are there too. I use those boxes for anything that I know I will need and do not want to find in the perpetual pile of "stuff" in the back-seat row of my truck. The bumper and boxes are light-weight aluminum. Aluminess is the company that makes them, and you can locate them online.

My cargo hauler, inserted into the truck's receiving hitch, is a beast. It is made by Let's Go Aero. I can haul an array of comforts there—coolers, cooking gear, you name it. Best thing? It slides out. Yep, I can slide the cargo basket back, allowing me to drop the tailgate no matter how full the hauler is. This is key when you need to get to your dogs on a long trip to give them water and also let them water the local shrubbery. I can then close the tailgate, push the cargo basket back into place, lock it down, and drive away. It really is a game-changer for long trips. I also have a roof rack, and they all work well when used properly.

Lastly is power. Goal Zero makes lots of battery and solar panel options. I have a Yeti 400 that I charge at home before I leave the house. It makes small work of charging GPS tracking collars for the dogs. Heck, in the interest of saving power, I have installed Microsoft Word on my cell phone and use a battery-powered keyboard that synchs up to my phone via Bluetooth. That previous sentence just strained the limits of my tech language, but I can do a lot of writing on the power carried by that Yeti 400 when I am only charging a cell phone rather than a laptop. The phone battery lasts longer in airplane mode. I can use the camera in airplane mode, take pictures and videos, and no one can call me. Battery lasts a long time.

Just last week, I was out in the field and got a phone call from my wife. "Hello?" I answered.

"Where have you been?"

"Running dogs," I said matter-of-factly.

"Your phone went right to voicemail," Renee said, "I just got done on a Zoom meeting, but you wouldn't know about Zoom.

"I know plenty about Zoom," I said.

"What do you know?"

"I just got a great video of my 10½-inch-tall beagle soloing a cottontail in really poor scent. And she was zooming!"

"Well," Renee said, "Your phone was turned off; I have been trying to call you."

"My phone was on. I was using it."

"No, you were not talking. It went straight to voicemail. You could not have silenced it that fast," Renee sighed.

"I was recording video of the zooming," I said, "I had the phone on airplane mode so no one could interrupt me."

"You figured out airplane mode?" she asked,

"I was born for social distancing. I am already at work, so overtime ain't gonna call me," I said.

"What are you talking about? You coming home soon? You have been gone for days."

"Yeah, but only because it is not hunting season. Or I might just stay out here . . ."

CORN TEEN

Around here, in rural Pennsylvania. Quarantine often gets pronounced as "corn teen." And that isn't the only linguistic anomaly here in the part of the state often maligned by outsiders by using the term Pennsyltucky. We drop Gs at the end of words, say "red up" to mean clean up, and say yinz as the second person plural. Pennsyltucky is most of the state, everything except Pittsburgh and Philadelphia, and a couple of smaller cities. I like Kentucky and Pennsyltucky, so they can call us whatever they want. My wife, Renee, is having a harder time than I was dealing with quarantine. She works full-time at Penn State and has been doing that from home lately. She is a people person. She is such a people person that she thinks everyone else must be, too. One of the best things about corn teen is that I no longer have to blame the dogs when I miss these play dates that she creates.

I have always been the kind of guy who can run dogs by myself and hunt rabbits by myself and be happy doing that. I have a few friends I hang out with once in a while, but I tend to find the social aspect of my vocation to be draining. For instance, hospital and nursing home visits are very much the intentional insertion of a pastor into the difficult situations that people are facing in order to help out. When I go do a hospital visit and see someone who is really sick, I find that to be a very draining process. Don't hear me saying that I do not like doing it or that I avoid it. No, I take this part of my job very seriously, but when it is done, I like to be able to retreat into my solitude for renewal. Maybe just me and the dogs in the field or a quiet supper at home with my wife.

Renee, by contrast, gains energy from being around people. She can float like a butterfly in and out of conversations at a large gathering. I will be in the corner talking to the other hunters and ignoring everyone else. In pre-COVID-19 times, she liked to think I needed new friends and scheduled these "play dates" where she made reservations with her friends and their husbands to meet at a restaurant and engage in small talk over food. Small talk isn't my thing. I often blame the dogs for missing these meals.

"Sorry, babe," I call her on the phone when the dogs are chasing a rabbit right past me so she can hear them. "These dogs are just pounding the rabbit. I lost track of time, and now I am having trouble catching them. I will be late, but I will make the supper. What restaurant do I go to?" At his point, I hope the pack doesn't lose the rabbit and end the hound music, which is a big part of my cover for the excuse I am fabricating.

"Are you showing up in coveralls again?" she seethes.

"I will put a shirt over top, so it looks like pants."

I usually arrive just in time to eat an appetizer as they are finishing up their main course; the dogs snooze in the dog box in the bed of my truck as I make enough small talk to get me through the encounter. It happens so much that her friends think I am some kind of professional trainer of beagles. HA!

In these corn teen times, I have been taking dogs afield twice per day, as doing visits is off-limits. I have been saving gas money by avoiding the beagle clubs and training dogs at my local hunting spots. This also allows me to avoid the old-timers who have been going to the beagle club a lot. The last thing I want to do is pass this bug to them. Restaurants have been closed, so we are eating at home all the time with no one else. While listening to hound dog music, I contemplate a faith-based offering that I can put on Facebook each day and generate ideas for our online worship services. Hey, in some ways, this has been easy for me. I take care of pastoral care by making a few phone calls to people each day.

The other day, the wind was howling, and most of the state was under a tornado watch. Rather than take dogs afield,

I decided to play some hymns on my mountain dulcimer and work from home. I did a little writing. Then, I decided to work on converting insight from academic commentaries and publications about a bible passage into a sermon—something a little less dry than a commentary. Some wit, a story or two to illustrate something intellectual and a weekly research paper gets changed into a sermon. Maybe it isn't much more interesting than the academic stuff, but hey, I try. When I am working on a passage from home, my wife thinks that I am not working.

"What are you doing?" Renee will ask.

"Working," I answer.

"Ha! Looks to me like you are laying on the couch and listening to music."

"I am thinking."

"Yeah, well, come watch me and see what work really looks like!"

Anyway, as the wind howled outside and the dogs were at attention anytime the screen door heaved against the doorknob latch, and the limbs from the trees in the yard shed twigs that were sent hurling into the house, I heard someone. It was this pleasant, jovial, affable, accommodating voice coming from the kitchen. She sounded so helpful. My first thought was that we are supposed to be practicing social distancing and no one should be in the house—why do we have company? My second thought was, how did this gal get into my house to see Renee without my beagle security system notifying me? They barked at car doors 100 yards from the house, and they had been barking at the wind all day. How could this intruder get past them? So, I walked into the kitchen to see who had dropped by. It was Work Renee.

Work Renee looks exactly like my wife. Except she is kind, gracious, and always willing to help. I have seen her be as patient as you can imagine when helping some tenured professor at the University do something to convert a traditional classroom course into an online project. Work Renee oozes compassion and will explain the same thing four, five, or even six times to a coworker. What do you think happens to me if I cannot hear something she says and ask her to repeat it once? I get the growl from Wife Renee, a very different person than Work Renee.

Lately, Work Renee has been on the phone and the computer, working from home. Her workload has doubled. She expends this great burst of gracious, gregarious helpfulness, and when all civility has been drained from her at the end of her day, she transforms into my wife. She has no sympathy then, when I can't do very difficult things like find a particular pair of boots, locate something in the refrigerator, or remember the password to the internet.

So, the best thing for me to do is get out of her way. I wake her up in the morning and make coffee. Then, I load up hounds and go to the woods. I work on some little things that I can share with the congregation and return home. I hear the pleasantness as she works, and then, around supper time, the transformation. When her computer is turned off, her voice hardens. Her vocabulary diminishes. She breaks out a few words with just four letters.

"Hey!" she yelled at me a few weeks into the corn teen after supper.

"Yes, sweetie?" I answered.

"Is it just me, or are you wearing pajamas and bib coveralls and that is it?" Renee asked, in a tone that meant she was not happy.

"Well," I scratched my chin, "I think th—"

"Stop touching your face!!"

"Sorry," I put my hands on my lap, "It isn't pajamas or bibs. It is either pajamas or bibs over pajamas."

"You've had the same pajamas on for days."

"Well, I am changing underwear and socks."

"That's disgusting."

"Hey," I said, "You put on a fancy shirt every day and do your makeup and hair, but you are totally in pajama bottoms for those online meetings that you are attending."

"They are different pajamas each day," she sneered in the way she does to point out the obvious.

"Prove it," I said, "You have 20 pairs of grey yoga pants." Just then, her phone rang.

"This is work!" she growled, "What do they want at this hour?"

"I don't know," I said.

She held her index finger up to me, indicating that I should be silent. "This is Renee," she answered with kindness oozing from her voice. The transformation is faster than when Bruce Banner becomes The Hulk. I pulled some bibs over my jammies, pulled my boots on, and loaded a few dogs to go to the field. Did the dogs I left at home get loud when they saw me break out the tracking collars and take a couple of dogs out to the truck? Oh, yeah. Renee had to go into the back yard, on the phone, as I took dogs out the front door just so no one heard the protests of the older hounds I didn't take. Old dogs run morning, youngsters in the evening. Stay socially distant and spiritually connected during this time of corn teen.

Exclusive

Do you ever feel good about being alone? I think that is how I tend to spend my rabbit hunting season when I run dogs almost exclusively by myself. Everyone else is archery hunting, grouse hunting, or fishing. Not many of us hunt rabbits. There are a few. There is a local guy who tends to follow me and try to steal my hunting spots. Let's be honest; my truck isn't exactly hard to notice. One day, I was trying to figure out how to give him the slip, and I remembered something that proved to be quite useful.

Many years ago, I visited a church member at the hospital and prayed with him before leaving the room. His roommate had a guest, too, and it was an older guy who chased me down to ask if I was a pastor. I said that I was, and he told me he was a lay speaker at his church and filled in for his church when the pastor was on vacation. He also filled in for many other churches when the pastor was away, and he did hospital visits every day for the churches because he was retired. It was a good talk, and I was glad to hear how active he was. Every time he saw me after that, I got to hear his most recent sermon. The whole thing. They were a half hour each. He found me one day, "Hey, I saw you get in the elevator as I was starting down the hall. Saw from the lights on the first floor that you got off at the 9th floor, so I thought I would look for you. He sat by the elevator until I was finished with my visit so he could give me his most recent sermon. I was getting on the elevator one day, pressed 14 for the 14th floor, and when the door was closing, I heard him yell my name. I looked at my shoes and let the doors shut. I was giddy; I was so excited to ditch him (I know that is terrible).

Remembering the ambush on the 9th floor a month earlier, I hit the button for the 10th floor, just to make him think that is where I was going! I excluded him that day, and it felt good, though I feel bad now. But, I was able to give him the slip by pretending to go somewhere that I was not going—the 10th floor. That event gave me an idea. Every time I saw his vehicle behind me, I would go to a spot that was public land, and while each spot where I led him was very different from one another—some were hilly, others were creek bottoms, some were full of big pines, and others had oaks—they all had one thing in common: They were amongst the places of highest deer density that I know, and I have never shot a rabbit at any of them.

I would put my dogs on the ground, walk them into the cover, and wait to peer through the trees to see his vehicle creep away. I would then load up the dogs and vamoose to a good spot. Hey, if you want to hunt with me, then ask, but don't try to follow me around and steal a spot.

Another thing that I am careful to do is not co-opt a spot from an invite. What do I mean by that? My friend Mike Leaman has a fantastic spot that he found, and got permission from the landowners to hunt. It is an Amish farm, and Mike asked the farmer, "Hey, should I stop by every time I hunt?"

"Nope," the landowner said, "Probably the less we talk, the better, just go ahead and hunt." Here is the thing. The farm is way closer to where I live than where Mike lives. He found it while staying at his camp. It would never occur to me that I ought to go there without him. I could probably go there a couple of times per year, and he would never know about it. I know what it is like to have someone be a guest at a spot that you went to all the work to find and then discover that they have returned to shoot as many rabbits as possible. Not my style.

About ten years ago, I was talking to a guy at a field trial here in Pennsylvania. He was all excited because he still had not killed a hare. We have a limited hare season in Pennsylvania.

"Where are you looking?" I asked him.

"Well," he said, "Up towards Ridgway."

"Well, what does that mean?" I asked.

"It's not too many miles away from Ridgway."

"I would go further north than that if I were you."

"Well, it is further north."

"Okay, well, tell me where you have been and what you know how to find," I said and "I will try to give you a spot close by that has a few hares."

"Well," It isn't a spot you would know."

"Look!" I said, "I grew up there. I walked dogs a half mile on a leash from my house and ran hare as a kid. I spent more time in The Allegheny National Forest than most kids did at the playground. I was just trying to help you. I am sure you will get your first hare eventually in a spot somewhere near Ridgway. I don't need to help you." I suppose, in his mind, he was trying to protect a spot from me, even though I doubt he, as a visitor, was as familiar with the area as I was from growing up there. I did get out a map and give him a good spot the next time I saw him.

Andy Purnell and I hunted together. A lot. We would get out in the thickets in the morning and bust the brush. Well, I would intercept rabbits in the brush. Andy stood on a dirt road with a .410 pistol. If the rabbit crossed the road, and if it was within range of that pistol, and if he had the pistol ready, he might shoot at it. Sometimes, he would kill one. Usually, he would call me a few days after I shot some rabbits.

"You make any rabbit stew from those rabbits you shot where we went hunting?" he would text me in the evening.

"Not yet. I can."

"Cool. Bring me some to work for lunch tomorrow."

I would get up and get the crockpot perking and start cutting vegetables. He worked at Lion Country Supply, and that was always a short detour for me. Hardly a day goes by that I do not have to go to Tyrone Hospital, or Altoona Hospital, or State

College Hospital, or all of them. I would stop in and give him the stew, and we would shoot the breeze about hunting until the phone lines got overwhelmed. "I gotta go help answer the lines," he would say, "Let's hunt tomorrow morning before work."

It wasn't until Andy died that I realized he lied to me all those years about being late for work. "Andy," I would ask, "Don't you have to be at work in five minutes?"

"Yeah," Andy would say, listening to our dogs.

"Dude," I would step in front of him to interrupt the hound dog trance he was in. He would snap out of it, and I would continue, "Andy, if we left right now, we are 40 minutes from the store. We still have to get the dogs."

"Bob, I work for a hunting dog store," Andy would say with the most convincing sincerity, "I am allowed to be late in hunting season. It is my job. Take your time, and try to kill that rabbit; it doesn't seem to want to cross this road. I will wait here in case you turn it." I would enter the thickets, and Andy would enter his hound trance. It doesn't seem like it has been five years since he died. Andy had a lot of friends. A whole lot. And they all have told me about secret spots that Andy had only shared with them. Whenever they tell me about a spot, I smile. It is one that I know. Always. There are a few places that no one mentions, spots that I have hunted with Andy. For five years, I have not gone to them. They were his spots. This year, I went to a couple of them for the first time since he died.

I am not really stealing them from him. And I kind of think he would want me to hunt them. Heck, I even stood on the dirt road and waited to shoot there like he would. I didn't see anyone else there. I am not sure that anyone else knew those spots. I have never said, "Hey, I got this spot that Andy only shared with me." But I think I could say that with truth about a couple of spots.

I told the story about Andy claiming that he was encouraged to be late for work during hunting season at his funeral. His boss was there, and he laughed until he cried. After the funeral,

I asked him if it was hard to get the day's work done when he let guys start late if the early morning hunting was going well.

"He wasn't allowed to be late," Buck said, "He just didn't care. What was I going to do? Yell at him? He wouldn't care about that either. And he was so good at tech support for the GPS collars. Man, he made the store a lot of money. We are closed right now for this funeral. The whole company is off work to come here and pay respects to Andy if they want. No one is even answering the phones. Andy was a big deal to our company. A real dog, man." The store had never shut down like that before.

Five years ago, that was. I was thinking about that as I hunted one of Andy's spots all by myself during the last week of the season. It is an exclusive spot. I tend to think of myself as an inclusive guy, and I like people to feel included. I guess when I am running dogs, I tend to be exclusive—not in the sense of being elite, but more like an attempt to be solitary and let that hound music trance do what it does to us. Field trial season is upon us now, and I will break out of my hunting solitude.

Looking forward to seeing everyone again.

INSTITUTIONALIZED

Well, here we are at the most romantic time of the year—Valentine's Day. In ancient, pre-Christian Rome, there was a festival that lasted from February 13-15 called Lupercalia. They would sacrifice goats and a dog. This was thought to purify the city and bring health and fertility. There was a big celebration of breastfeeding, much like you see when soccer moms gather in coffee shops today to talk about breastfeeding so loudly that everyone knows that they had extracted a couple of pints of milk for the baby that they dropped off at daycare.

Anyway, the ancient festival would also offer cakes as a sacrifice. These cakes were made by a whole bunch of virgin women called Vestal Virgins. They remained virgins for 30 years after being inducted at about the age of 10, and then they retired at the age of 40ish with a full pension. It was considered a great honor to marry one of them, and noblemen would compete for the right. So, after the animals were killed at the altar, two priests would then anoint their foreheads with blood left on the knife from the sacrifice. That would then be washed away with a wool rag soaked in milk. These two priests would then laugh at each other, which must have been creepy. Next, strips of the hide (they were called Februa, from which we get the word February) and these strips of goat hide would be carried by young men who ran naked in a circle around a hill. They slapped people with those bloody strips, and this was thought to help women get pregnant or make the pregnancy go well. That was Lupercalia. Later, we get Valentine's Day at the same time of year, which makes all of that stuff look somewhat normal. Well, maybe not normal, but let's face it: Valentine's Day drives people crazy.

Me, I try not to get too excited. All you really need to do is send flowers. If your wife works with other women, it is best to send the flowers there. If she gets a bunch of them delivered in front of all the other gals, then you will have made a good show. It is also important to take her out to supper as well. Here is how that is done best: make a reservation a few weeks in advance. But make it for eight o'clock. When it comes time to take your wife for supper, you simply say, "Whew, I really had to pull some strings to get reservations, but we have them. Tonight, at eight." My wife, Renee, then goes to work thrilled that I was able to get a reservation on such a busy day. But did you see what I did there? Waiting until eight o'clock means that I can hunt until dark!

Alright, now that is a veteran move. If you are a Newlywed, that may not work. You will have to test the waters. But once you have some years of service, you can get by with hunting a few hours in the afternoon and meeting her later. I once officiated a wedding, and the gal who played the guitar for this outdoor wedding was very talented. She writes her own songs and sings. She almost made it on TV for American Idol. She just had to win one more contest, or whatever it is called. I don't watch the show, but it was all over our local news.

Anyway, after I pronounced them married, they kissed, and we sent the bride and groom marching down the outdoor aisle, which was a mowed path. I looked at the musician and indicated that she should play some sort of recessional music. She launched into a very good cover, which she totally owned, and made it her own. She strummed a few chords, and I thought, "No" to myself since I knew the song, but she did perform a fantastic rendition of Johnny Cash's "Folsom Prison Blues." I shrugged my shoulders and enjoyed the song.

"Sorry," she said, "I do not know many love songs."

"Meh," I answered. Prison. Marriage, they are both institutions and leave you institutionalized."

If you are not institutionalized, then you will not get away with hunting on Valentine's Day. Your wife needs to have other married friends for enough years that she realizes that spending time in the woods chasing rabbits is not the worst behavior that a man can display. She needs enough years of matrimony to hear about all the stuff her friends deal with in their marriage. Staying out late at night, chasing other women, that kind of stuff. Once you have been married a dozen years or more, she will have no trouble with you going to the woods. Being late for rabbit reasons becomes virtuous in comparison.

"Say honey bunny," I said last year on Valentine's Day, "Since we aren't able to eat the fancy steak dinner until eight o'clock, would it be alright if I hunted the last couple hours of daylight? I will come home right after, wash up, and we can go eat."

"Yes, go ahead," Renee said, "Oh, and I picked up those .410 shells that were on sale at the mall. I was looking for gloves and saw a good price. I put them on your desk."

"Well," I said, "Happy Valentine's Day to me." That, my friends, is fully institutionalized. She went to work and got flowers. Am I saying that I pulled one over on Renee? Nah, she probably knows. February 14 isn't the only day that I hunt the last hour of daylight. I do it quite a bit. And there are some things that you can do to help out even more. When we first married, my refrigerator wasn't domestic. It was mostly mustard and hot sauce. Maybe five of each. And the fishing bait was on the top shelf (hey, the bottom was too cold). That was in September when we married. In the fall, she comes home to a common sight—dead rabbits soaking in a little salt water. Yep, right there on the top shelf. All these years later, it is no trouble now, but in our first hunting season, she wasn't fond of the sight. Especially if it was a great day afield, and I had her favorite Tupperware container filled with rabbit meat right where she could see it. What was my solution? I bought a dorm fridge advertised as being for sale in May when the college kids went home. I got my own fridge for bait and bunnies—and it was viewed as the kindest thing I could have done!

Here is the last thing that makes the day go well. You have to get one of those blank greeting cards. There's a bunch in my house because Renee went through a phase where she was making homemade cards for people. For all occasions. Congratulation cards for any achievement, get-well cards, birthday cards (of course) graduation cards, and many more. In case your wife doesn't make cards, it is basically an art project that takes four hours, and Lord knows how much paper, glue, glitter, stamps, and stickers. There is no cost savings, as I believe each card has a minimum of $10 worth of materials. All the glue and glitter means that it will be cheaper to put the thing in a priority mail envelope than to pay for regular stamps. They are way too heavy for one stamp.

Don't worry about the glitter or anything. Just get a blank card from a store, and then write your own Valentine. It doesn't have to be that good. It doesn't have to rhyme. It is, however, one of those things where quantity matters as much as quality. I just write all the things that Renee does to make me happy. Sometimes, you have to begin thinking about these things the day before to get a long enough list. Tiny things work. "You make the best pie" is okay. She is always noticing the tiny things (good and bad) in me, and so I notice all her good things.

See, and here is the thing: when five o'clock rolls around, and it is time to get hungry, she will be home waiting while you are finishing up the hunt. When you leave for the hunt, you have to leave this card where she will find it. She will be delighted. This then lets you be a little late getting home if you hunted a good spot a bit further from home. Leave the card with one fancy chocolate bar. One candy bar is good—you buy the biggest box of candy you can find, and she will think you are calling her heavy. One. Expensive. Chocolate. That is it. She will eat it while reading the card.

I was sharing all this with a young man recently, who got married this past summer.

"Man," he said, "How did you learn all that?"

In my best imitation of Morgan Freeman from *Shawshank Redemption*, I said, "Young man, I have been thoroughly institutionalized. And it ain't all bad."

Miss Communication

"How long have you been married?" I was asked by a guy while rabbit hunting.

"Well," I said, "A few months ago, my wife was away for a two-week business trip. I picked her up at the airport at eight p.m., and before she told me that she missed me or anything, she asked me if we could go to a restaurant since she had been on a plane over the supper hour."

"What did you say?" the guy asked me.

"I told her that I already ate supper, but I could eat a small snack. Then she told me that she loved me."

"Ha!" he laughed.

When it comes to marriage, some things are just realities, and when you have hunting beagles, it can get even more complex. For instance, my wife, Renee, now accepts that there will be dismembered rabbits in the fridge, soaking in salt water, for many of the days in November, December, January, and February. Was it easy when we first got married?

"What in the world is that?" I remember being asked the first time it happened, a few months after our wedding.

"Three rabbits soaking in water with a little salt. I will freeze them in a couple of days."

Years later, she routinely moves the rabbits around. I use quart spaghetti jars, Tupperware containers, or even empty plastic containers that held the Chinese takeout food. "I put the rabbits from today behind the rabbits from Wednesday. Make sure you freeze those first. I will cook the rabbits stored in the in the door tonight," is the sort of thing that Renee will often say to me now. But we took a few years to get to this point!

Do we still have misunderstandings? Yeah. Often, it is because I am not paying attention. Now, don't get me wrong, I am not trying to ignore her; it is just that I often don't understand what she is talking about. She does a lot of work on the computer, and most of that stuff eludes me. One time, a person in her department had to be taught how to make a PDF file. She talked the guy right through the process. She was so kind and sweet. She will help me, too, but often, I get sharper comments from her. "I can help you, but not right now. You have to wait!" Then, she turns on the sweetness and helps somebody do a really easy thing on their computer, talking them through the whole thing. Then I called her back in a few hours, "Hey, did you forget about me?"

"Just unplug it and turn it back on," she said.

"I thought you said that was not the proper thing to do," I said,

"It isn't. But sometimes it is the only thing that works."

Anyway, when she is talking to me about servers and internet connections at her office and how bad things went, I often just do not know what she is talking about. Oh, and I have learned the hard way that asking for clarification, which seems like a good way to show interest, actually frustrates her because she can't believe how stupid I really am.

And offering old fashioned ideas is no help either.

"UGH!" she said after supper one night.

"What is wrong?"

"This link is not working, and I am trying to set up an online meeting for tomorrow."

"Oh," I said, "Does everyone work in the same building?"

"Yes," she said as she hammered on the computer keys.

"Then why don't you just meet in a room?" I suggested. She looked at me like I was a complete moron.

"It makes sense to me," I said.

"Well," she looked at me over her glasses, "That won't work because we have to share files and analyze them."

"Or you could print the files and have them in the room for everyone to see."

"Oh yeah?" Renee said, "Would we do that while we watched a presentation with a VCR?" I didn't realize she was being sarcastic.

"You guys still have a VCR?" I said, "Nice. Don't you miss going to the video rental store and looking for a movie to watch?"

"Why? You can now look at all the movies on the television screen and pick one. Never have to leave the house."

"Yeah," I said, "I know. They got rid of all the fun."

So, I zone out when she is talking jargon and mumbo jumbo. I do not ask her to explain terms. I do not give ideas. I just nod my head a lot and say things that indicate that I am aware she is talking.

So, recently, I was out in the field with a pair of beagles and really had a good hunt. The chases were going great, I was getting good shots, and the beagles were sounding awesome. My cell phone rings. I was waiting for the rabbit. I looked at it and saw it was Renee. She was on a trip for work. The phone was on vibrate, and I did not want to talk and spook the bunny. I ignored it. The rabbit comes around in a bit, and I miss the shot. I saw it too late; it was beyond me and offered no shot other than in the back. I relocated for another opportunity. Buzz buzz buzz, the phone rings again. Renee. I actually silenced the phone this time. I shot the rabbit and called her back.

"What's up?" I asked.

"Did you not get my text that I was landing early today?"

"Today?" I asked. My calendar says tomorrow.

"I told you on the phone the other day that I was coming home a day early. I told you that I was landing today at five o'clock.

"Oh, yeah, that's right," I lied after I looked at my phone and saw that it was only nine o'clock in the morning. I will be there early."

"Early? You are late. I texted you yesterday that my flight changed, and I will be at the airport by eight o'clock this morning!"

"You did?"

"Yes!!"

"You want the good news or the bad news?" I asked.

"I am sure the bad news is that you are hunting since it is a Saturday morning in hunting season," Renee sighed.

"Hey, you are good. Really bright. But your job already knows that. That is why you have to travel so much."

"Stop the kissing up. What's the good news?"

"I am at a hunting spot close to the airport, so I can pick you up in just about a half hour or so.

"Wonderful," she said.

"Say, hon," I paused to think of something to say, "I bet you were flying during breakfast time. I bet we can get right into a breakfast place easy right now; the early morning rush is over."

"Today is Saturday, so right now is the rush," Renee replied.

"I'm going to hang up and come get you."

"That would be wonderful."

I whisked over there and got her luggage loaded and she jumped into my truck.

"I can't believe you didn't get my text about the flight change."

I handed her my phone. "Is it there?"

She scrolled through the messages. "You have like 20 unopened texts in here."

"Group texts," I said, "I get lost in those. Too many texts that are just a thumbs up sign."

"Here," she said, "I texted you at four o'clock yesterday."

"I was hunting then," I said, "It is hard to text in the winter. My hands get cold."

"What about all these pictures you take of beagles chasing and dead rabbits and videos of beagles retrieving rabbits?"

"My hands get really cold!" I said, "But the pictures are nice."

"I will get you a pair of gloves that work on a phone touch screen. Then you can answer my texts if I am in a meeting and can't call you," she said.

"Do you really think that is going to make me text more?"

"Probably not."

"Want to stop at the Waffle Shop? I will buy late breakfast."

"I love you."

If I am honest, she gives me all the information in texts, email, or some other electronic way. She gives me more than I can keep up with. She is Miss Communication, but in my brain, it all becomes miscommunication sometimes. I think I have a VCR in storage somewhere . . .

BLINKITY BLANKING

When I think of Thanksgiving, I always think about two perennial truths in life. One is that you can't make everybody happy. My grandmother would not eat turkey—not a wild turkey that we might shoot or even a tame one from the store either. No, there was only one thing that she would want for the big feast, and that was a capon. Now, if you are unfamiliar with a capon, it is basically the poultry equivalent of a gelding or a steer. I have never researched the matter, but somehow, someway, some people take the time to castrate a rooster. The birds get a bit lazy and plump after that. You can't find these things just any old place.

"Why does gram insist on a capon every year?" I asked my Dad, "Wouldn't a great big store-bought chicken be just as good?"

"Well," Dad scratched his five o'clock shadow, which tended to arrive by noon, "For as long as I have known your mother, it seems to me that her Mom has always wanted a capon. I think maybe she would emasculate all males in all places if she had her way." Only Dad didn't say emasculate. I am sure you can guess what he said.

"Where are we gonna find one this year?" I asked.

"I don't get involved with that," Dad said.

"Last year, we drove an hour to find one," I said.

"I think they can be special ordered at the butcher shop, if they call it in time," Dad said. This was back when butcher shops still could be found. *Five and Dime* stores still populated small towns, too, where, as a kid, I could get a Matchbox car for one dollar. *Western Auto* part stores still existed, too, and a guy could buy parts and fix his own car. This was back before cars had computers. Anyway, the butcher shop would give away chicken wings to people because the folks in Buffalo may have been putting hot sauce on them, but the trend hadn't caught fire across the nation yet. Regular customers of a butcher shop would readily be given wings for free if you mentioned that you would be making chicken noodle soup.

"Did they order the capon yet?" I asked.

"I don't know," Dad said, "Hey, Hon, did you order that blinkity blanking neutered bird for your Mom yet?" Only he didn't say blinkity blanking. Or neutered.

"It is coming on Friday!" Mom yelled from the kitchen, "But I could only get it in Bradford!"

"Bradford?!" Dad yelled back.

"Yeah, and I have to take Mom the opposite way to a doctor's appointment on Friday. Can you pick it up? It is your long weekend!"

Not only was this back when five and dime, *Western Auto*, and butcher shops existed, but it was when there were still lots of factories that made things right here in America. My Dad was employed by a factory, a paper mill, and he worked on a tour schedule. He changed shifts every week, rotating counter-clockwise, from 7-3 to 11-7 to 3-11 and then back to 7-3 again. His days off always changed each week, too and were almost never on a weekend. This whole schedule could be subject to change if overtime were offered, if someone got sick, or if guys swapped shifts for whatever reason. An entire calendar was kept in the kitchen so that we could figure out how to schedule certain events around Dad's work. Periodically, he would get the elusive long weekend, which was Friday and Saturday off for one week, and Sunday and Monday off for the start of the next week. However, he would have to go in Monday night at 11 o'clock.

Dad heard Mom's request for him to go get the blankity blanking chicken. But he pretended not to hear.

"Can you?" Mom popped her head around the corner into the living room and looked right at him. Dad wasn't a go-to-the-store kind of guy. In fact, he had never deposited his paycheck at the bank, at least not that I ever saw. Mom would take it in and deposit all but $10, and Dad would then get the ten-dollar bill to buy a case of beer for the week. The only stores I ever saw him enter were the beer distributor, the lumber yard, the gasoline station, and the hardware store. Oh, and *Western Auto*. He had one blank check in his wallet if he needed to make a big purchase.

"Really?" Dad asked, "Friday is still almost a week from Thanksgiving. Can't you get there before Thanksgiving?"

"Sometimes they won't hold them if they have a kid working the store. They don't get that many delivered."

"You want to skip school and go rabbit hunting on Friday?" Dad looked at me.

"Um, yeah!" I said.

"Do you have any tests on Friday?" Mom asked.

"Hmm," I cocked my head to the side and pretended to be in deep thought, trying to recall my schedule, "Nope, but I do have two on Thursday this week." The lie rolled off my tongue with such ease, that it frightens me today.

"Okay," Mom said.

"If we are going there, can I get some of the homemade jerky they sell?" I asked.

"I don't give a blank," Dad patted me on the head. As I am sure you know, he didn't say blank. "Just as long as you go in the store and get the capon."

I wasn't old enough to hunt alone, so any day that I got to miss school and hunt was a good day. Because of the tour shifts, Dad was rarely off on the weekend. Much of the hunting season had me calling various relatives, trying to get someone to take me. Sometimes gram herself would do it and simply give me a lift to the hunting spot and sit in her car and knit until I was done. Fortunately, no game warden ever stopped me at those times because I am quite sure that the law required her to be a lot more hands-on than making a wool sweater a quarter mile away from me.

"What time are we leaving on Friday?" I asked.

"Let's leave early," he said. "I know a spot on the other side of Bradford that was logged a few years ago. We can try that."

We left early and dropped the dogs about daylight. It wasn't long until the dogs had a rabbit going, and it ran for a very short circle. As a young hunter, I was eager to get it and made fast work of that rabbit with my 20 gauge. It was a *Western Auto* brand gun, by the way.

"You in a rush?" Dad asked.

"I have to get three more before you shoot," I said. Dad never shot until I had my limit. We worked further into the clear-cut and near some hemlocks. The dogs were off and really flying.

"Oh no," I said as they ran out of hearing.

"Deer," Dad gritted his teeth.

We may have had *Western Auto* and free chicken wings, but back in those days, you had to catch a dog when it was chasing a deer. No "tone" button beeped a collar, and no stimulations to discipline a dog either.

"Want me to catch them?" I asked.

"Do you know where we are?" Dad asked.

"Not really."

"Stay here," he said. I waited for an hour. I got nervous. I walked into the woods in a straight line and yelled for Dad. I walked back to where I had been. I walked into the woods in a slightly different angle and yelled again. Then returned to the spot where I was supposed to wait. I did it a few more times. Then I heard Dad, "Come on, girl," he was calling to Princess, "You're a good girl! Good boy, Duke." This was odd because if he were going to discipline a dog, he would be "blinkity blanking" and not praising.

"What's going on?" I yelled.

"They were on a hare!" Dad yelled back, pleased about the matter.

"Really?" I asked.

"Yep," Let's get out of here and come back after Christmas when hare season opens.

"Okay," I said.

"What's in your vest?" he reached inside. "Whew, it's a cottontail. I didn't look earlier."

"Want to hunt somewhere else today?" I asked.

"Yeah," I know a nearby farm that should have a few cottons." We went and I got two more rabbits and missed one. I was too excited at the prospect of getting my limit and missed from the jitters. We went to get the capon and I came out with the bird in one hand and a massive piece of beef jerky and a bottle of Pepsi in the other.

"Poor fella," Dad laughed at the capon as he placed it into an old milk crate in the bed of the truck.

The second perennial truth that I recall about Thanksgiving is that it is nigh impossible for a mother and a daughter to both run the same kitchen for the same holiday meal. One has to be the boss. Dad and I always went rabbit hunting for Thanksgiving Day, just to avoid the endless debates that would ooze out of the kitchen. They couldn't agree on basting or seasoning or even whether to mash or whip the potatoes.

"Let's go!" Dad yelled up the stairs to me almost a week after we picked up the capon. His voice calling me to go hunting was a great way to start Thanksgiving. "Your gram is on the way!" I ran downstairs, loaded the dogs, and we headed for the briars. It was windy, and some sort of weather was moving in. It felt like snow, maybe. It wasn't cloudy yet, but you could see it would be doing something that night. Maybe rain. Maybe snow. Maybe in between. The Weather Channel didn't exist yet, and the meteorologists on the local news had to really understand the weather, and even with their training, they could make mistakes. Two different meteorologists could give very different predictions for the same area. This was decades before the supercomputers and simulation models that made the job of weather prediction more uniform and reliable as it is now. This was before the days of putting attractive gals with almost no training in meteorology in a tight dress and having them read the forecast.

We got two hole shots in an hour. A hole shot is when the rabbit runs less than 100 yards and goes straight underground into a groundhog hole. Impending weather often will cause a rabbit to not stay above ground. "You know what will not go in a hole?" Dad asked.

"What?" I asked.

"A hare."

"Never will go in one?" I questioned.

"Not very blanking often. Extremely rare."

"Interesting," I said.

"Wanna go run them? You won't be able to shoot them. The season isn't open."

"I don't know, I kinda want to hunt."

"You probably won't get much shooting today anyway, with the weather coming."

"Okay," I said.

We drove past Bradford and cut the dogs loose. They got a chase going easily. Dad and I walked around. "Okay," he said, "They crossed this logging road. Let's wait here. If it is a hare, they should cross near here again. For some reason, hare will cross a dirt road at the same spot sometimes." A half-hour later, they were back. We then just milled around, walking and listening to the dogs. Trying to get additional glimpses of the hare. It was almost 2/3 white, changing into the winter coat. I grew up in one of the few areas of Pennsylvania to have a decent population of hare. We talked about hunting, life, grandmothers, capons, missing school, and all the other topics that might pop into our heads.

"There's the hare!" Dad said and looked at his watch, "Almost two o'clock. They should be done arguing about the meal. This would be a good time to catch them." We walked down the dirt road and got ready to intercept the beagles. They were a long way behind it. Dad just stood there smiling.

"What's so funny?" I asked.

"Nothing."

"Why are you smiling?"

"I love that sound. Them blankers are really blanking rolling that blinker!" You know what he really said. Happy Thanksgiving.

Pumpkin Spice

Many years ago, I told the story of an event that got me ostracized by other clergy in our community. It was a church Halloween party, though they were afraid to call it Halloween. They wanted a Halloween party for the kids so the youngsters could wear costumes and get candy, but they did not want to call it Halloween for fear of it seeming evil. I forget what they called the gathering, but all the kids had to dress like bible characters. So, we had a bunch of kids dressed in bathrobes and sandals and carrying sticks. They all looked alike. It was kids from all over town all the churches were represented. I helped kids figure out how to go home with their parents and come back with their real costumes.

"Oh yeah, you can be a skeleton. If the other pastors ask, you just tell them that you are the dry bones of Ezekiel's vision," I said.

"Yeah, you can be a ghost. You are the ghost of Samuel, summoned by the witch at Endor."

"A witch? Sure, go get the costume and hang out with the ghost."

"A knight? Hmm. Tell them you are the Armor of God."

The important thing was that the kids could prove that they were Biblical characters. The other pastors figured out that I was helping the kids, but those kids had a blast wearing their trick-or-treat costumes. It was worth my being viewed as too secular by the strict pastors.

Speaking of trick or treat, that has always been the danger of Halloween at my house. Two dangers—firstly, a dog sneaking out of the house as candy is distributed (we started crating the beagles for the entire event), and secondly, dogs ingesting chocolate, which is poisonous to them. Yeah, I have heard plenty of stories about dogs ingesting chocolate and being fine, but the fact remains that it is poisonous to dogs. The darker the chocolate, the deadlier it is. The home remedy, as my vet once told me, is to feed a turkey baster of hydrogen peroxide to the pooch every few minutes. It takes two adults, minimum, to get this job done. The end result will be vomiting, which makes the puking scenes from *The Exorcist* look tame, though the color will be chocolatey brown instead of whatever it was in that movie. This year, the plan is to pass out candy from the porch, keeping all dogs sequestered from the candy. Well, most of it. My wife, Renee, always keeps a stash of "emergency chocolate" in the house somewhere. It is usually in a cabinet or drawer. This is for her stressful days at work. A scattered pile of wrappers in the garbage is the only evidence left behind to show how much stress may have plagued her that day.

Chocolate isn't her daily October indulgence. The big one would be pumpkin spice. Pumpkin spice, what? Everything. You name it, she finds it. Coffee, bread, tea, peanut butter, popcorn, and nutrition bars.

"Try this," I said to her; I took a bite first to prove it wasn't a prank.

"Hmm," she said, "What is it?"

"It is good, huh?" I took another bite.

"It is tasteless," Renee exclaimed.

"I just cut the flesh out of a pumpkin and baked it."

"All by itself?" she asked.

"Yeah," I took another bite."

"Why would you do that?"

"To prove that there is no such thing as pumpkin spice! No spice comes from the pumpkin!" I said, "It is just cinnamon and nutmeg, which you can get all year long."

"Anyone ever tell you that you take the fun out of the holidays?" Renee asked.

"I will have you know that I am quite jovial at a religious Halloween party. Except in the eyes of the other pastors."

Pumpkin cappuccino has been popular lately. Sometimes, in the evenings, Renee and I have been running dogs to get ready for the arrival of rabbit season. She will get her Cappuccino at the gas station on the way.

"Duke is slowing down," she said, sipping her pumpkin spice cappuccino as she offered her commentary of the chase.

"Well, he is nine years old now," I said, "He still looks good on a rabbit, just not all day."

"I like Blitz," she said.

"He runs well," I said. Reminds me of his Uncle Hoss." Hoss is Duke's littermate.

"Diamond is in the back," Renee said, poking me in the ribs with her left index finger while sipping pumpkin spice with her right hand. She knows I like Diamond.

"Well, she is tiny," I said, "But wait until they get into the thick blowdowns." Eventually, they did work the rabbit into that tangled mess, and tiny Diamond crawled on her belly and pushed the rabbit out the other side, leaving the other dogs behind her as they ran out of the brush to get to the front. "Did you see that?" I asked her.

"I did," Renee tipped her cup high to finish the cappuccino, "And now Blitz has the front again."

This difference of opinion continued for weeks. One Saturday morning we took dogs to a spot where we would not be able to pass a gas station. We brought coffee from home. "Look," I said, "I am not saying Blitz is bad. I like him a lot, but when the rabbits turn into brush rats that don't run very big, it is Diamond that saves the chase."

"I guess," she sipped her coffee."

"You sad because we couldn't get your cappuccino?"

"No," she smiled, "I have pumpkin spice creamer in our fridge."

"Or we could add nutmeg and cinnamon to milk," I said.

"It wouldn't be the same," she pointed at the dogs, "Who is that in the front?"

"Blitz," I sullenly agreed.

"You sound sad," Renee said, "Want some pumpkin spice?"

"Yuck," I stuck my tongue out.

"It can't taste as bad as your dog getting beaten by Blitz."

"C'mon," I said, "Duke just got that check. Diamond and Blitz are both Duke's pups. I like them all."

That night, I figured out her love of Blitz. "He is the cutest beagle of all!" she exclaimed as Blitz plopped onto her lap and rolled over for a belly rub.

"Oh," I said, "This is about cuteness, not accomplishment in the field?"

"Blitz is both better and cuter," She hauled him into the air to push her face against his.

"If you have been following my author page on Facebook, you will see that most of my readers would disagree. They think Diamond is the cuter of the two."

"She is just smaller. Look at Blitz!" she smothered the dog and covered his eyes with his own ears.

The next few trips afield were clearly Blitz-dominated. I told Renee that, too. "Well," I scratched my beard, "Blitz looked the best today."

"Again," she grinned.

"Why are you smiling? Because Blitz looked good?" I asked as I shifted gears.

"No. Because these pumpkin spice cookies rock!"

The next day, I was at work and got a text. It was a picture of Diamond wearing a costume. She was dressed up as a pumpkin.

"She is in costume!" the text from Renee read.

"I think clothes on dogs look stupid."

"She looks cute."

"Oh, you think cuter than Blitz?"

"No, but she is getting closer now."

"Should she be in a beagle-approved costume? Like the pastor approved Halloween party at church?"

"She is."

"Oh Yeah? What."

"She is a Snoopy-themed costume. Snoopy from Charlie Brown."

"Really? What is she?"

"She is The Great Pumpkin."

"I see…"

"But she is still not as great as Blitz!"

"If you say so. Want to run dogs tonight?"

"I don't know," Renee answered.

"I have pumpkin roll that a church member put in the office."

"I got time to watch Blitz run better than his sister."

CRUISING

I recently cashed a check and got a $100 bill. I hid it inside of my wallet, between my Driver's license and a business card. I keep it there to have enough gas money to get home, no matter what. You never know when a debit card's magnetic strip will stop working. The Benjamin hides out in my wallet, but sometimes my wife, Renee, will force me to use it, at some yard sale or odd place where she finds an antique or piece of furniture advertised. Typically, though, it sits in my billfold for emergencies, always at the ready for a couple of tanks of gasoline. At a church picnic, the topic of gasoline came up. One of the things that completely flabbergasts the contemporary teenager is stories about "cruising" with no particular place to go.

"So," one kid said to me at a church dinner, "You would drive around with no destination?"

"Correct," I answered.

"Well," he raised his right eyebrow in complete bewilderment, "How did you know when you got there?"

"When you got there, you knew."

"Where was there?"

"It could be anywhere?"

"Like where?"

"Maybe, the county fair."

"What would be there?"

"A funnel cake to share."

"With who, at the fair?"

"A date, you know, go as a pair."

"A funnel cake sounds rare!"

"Common carnival fare."

"Odd meal. Did she care?"

"It would not stain the shirt that she would wear."

"Would people watch you and stare?"

"Nah, 'cause back in the truck, we would go on another trip! Sometimes, we drove up and down the same street, main street, over and over, just looking to see who might be hanging out that night."

Ultimately, the youngsters got around to asking the question that was worth asking. "How much did gasoline cost then?"

"I think when my oldest friends started driving, it was like 80 cents per gallon. Maybe less," I said.

This, of course, brought complete astonishment to their faces, and they finally understood. "So," the youngster said, "It didn't cost much at all to go anywhere?"

"We would drive anywhere," I said, "All day long."

"Really?"

"If a few of us each kicked in a couple of dollars, there were times when a friend's car went home with more gas in the tank than when it left the house." That bit of trivia left them so speechless that you could have heard a nickel drop, which is what happened. "We would find coins, like that one," I continued, "In couch cushions or the laundry, and could buy enough gasoline to go wherever we might need to be." Anywhere was endless. It was a bunch of somewhere. And nowhere. That was the beauty of going anywhere."

When I was able to drive at 16, I would often take beagles into the hills behind my home to run them. I could walk there, but I was permitted to take the truck up a steep logging road to make it easier after I was old enough to drive. At that time, hares were common in northern Pennsylvania. If you spent a lot of time in the woods, you would find them. They were the most common critter that were never seen by people who stuck close to town. In the early fall, before we could start hunting rabbits, we tried to get the dogs on hare to make up for the lack of exercise that was common in the humid month of August. "We would go into the hemlocks and cut the dogs loose right before dark," I was telling a young rabbit hunter.

"Did the coyotes come in?"

"Nah, there weren't any coyotes then."

"No coyotes at all?"

"Nope. Most dangerous encounter in them days was porcupines."

"Wow, you are older than coyotes?"

"Ha! No, we just never had any here in the east."

"Could you see the dogs at night?"

"Not really," I said, "So we just built a small fire, ate some food, and listened to the dogs whenever they got close and within hearing. Sometimes, they would run a big woods cottontail rabbit and stay closer to the fire. Sometimes, they would go way out of hearing, and we had no idea where they were. We would lie on the ground and listen."

"Did the ticks bite you?"

"I never saw a tick back then. I certainly never saw deer ticks. Maybe a couple of dog ticks. If it got too late, we would have to find the dogs."

"You couldn't track them?"

"No," I said, "Back then, all of the satellites were celebrities. They only ever were seen on TV, being pushed out of the Space Shuttle."

"What did the satellites do?"

"I guess they spied on the Russians. Otherwise, astronauts just walked around in space on a fancy rope working on them. Once in a while, you would hear about one falling to earth. There were no satellites tracking dog collars back then."

"How did you find the dogs?" the kid asked.

"Sometimes, I said, "You had to leave your hunting coat on the ground and trust that the dog would find it. Sometimes, the dog would follow my tracks home, and it would be in the yard when I woke up. So, even though I was allowed to drive to the woods, sometimes I walked."

"Really?"

"Yes. Haven't you noticed that even at the beagle club, I walk around a little bit and leave a scent trail back to the truck?"

"That seems weird; we just let the dogs out and sit on the tailgate."

"I know, but that is how it was in the old days."

"Could you hit the tone button to get the dogs to come in?"

"There wasn't a tone button then. You had to yell really loud. Or whistle loud."

"How loud can you whistle?"

I blasted a note or two, whistling with my fingers.

"How did you learn that?" the kid said, covering his ears.

"It took me two days of practice almost nonstop. I watched my Dad do it to call the dogs when they had lost a rabbit. We just walked around the woods, and he whistled. Eventually, they heard us and came. I was so jealous that I practiced until I got it figured out. Gave me the worst headache of my life."

After the church picnic, everyone went home. That evening, my wife, Renee, was asking me about going to do a little shopping.

"Where do you want to go?"

"I just need a few groceries and cleaning supplies."

"Sounds good," I said, "What store?"

"Do you need anything? We could go to supper too. We can go anywhere."

"Cripes," I said, "Do you know how much gas money it costs to go anywhere now?"

"What are you talking about?" she said.

"Don't worry. I have enough gas money to get anywhere," I thought about the $100 bill, "I just don't know if it is enough to get home from there." She looked at me like I made no sense at all, but I was getting used to that.

DECISION FATIGUE

For years, my wife, Renee, and I lived in two separate houses. Well, to be more precise, we each served a parish that owned their parsonage. That was how we were living while dating before we got married. We never really consolidated our stuff. When we married, my stepson, Wesley, was still in elementary school, so rather than make him leave his friends and change school districts, we stayed in the parsonage where she was serving. Plus, it is a bigger house. Now, to be sure, I was still staying at "my house." I stayed there on Saturday nights, any night that I had a meeting and any night that I might have to be there particularly early. I stayed there for all of deer season and some days in rabbit season, too.

The bishop decided to do some realigning of churches, and in order to make room for a new pastor, they moved Renee out of her residence and into mine. We've been married almost 14 years and never had to live together every day and every night. When she got mad at Wesley, she would say, "Go to your room!" When she got mad at me, she would say, "Go to your house." She moved into my house a couple of months ago. Her commute is now 45 minutes to get to her day job, at Penn State.

"Get up, sweetie," I said to her as I sipped coffee from a travel mug one morning after she moved in. She hates waking up. I always add the sweetie if I wake her.

"What time is it?"

"It is five-thirty in the morning. I sipped my beverage, "I just loaded the dogs, and I am going to take them to the woods. I won't be here to make sure that you don't turn off your alarm clock."

"I can't get up right now," she squinted as I turned on the light, "I slept on my arm, and my hand fell asleep."

"Did it cut off blood flow to your legs too?"

"No."

"Stand up; you will get circulation back faster.

"You don't have to be a jerk. I can't move till my hand wakes up."

"That can't be true."

"Go run dogs."

Another odd thing about the reverse commute, where she drives and has to come home, is supper. If she has evening meetings, then I am cooking supper, or we are eating separately. It all depends on how late she will be getting home.

"I'll cook," I said one night, "What do you want?"

"I can't decide."

"Want to skip supper then?"

"No! But I have decision fatigue."

"What? You made that up."

"It is real. It is caused by having to make too many decisions. Like I do all day long. Then, when faced with a question of limitless possibility, you freeze up."

"That sounds phony. Like not being able to stand if your hand falls asleep,"

"It is real."

"Okay," I said, "So now what?"

"I just want you to decide, and I know you will do great. Whatever you pick will be fine." We end the call.

Anyone who is married can tell that this is a trap. She has just lied to me. I thought about it and decided that I would go with mashed potatoes. My wife has had dreams about mashed potatoes. She fell asleep on the couch and was moaning and groaning in her dreams.

"What's going on, honey?" I asked.

"Mmmm," she was smiling and talking in her sleep.

"What is it?" I asked.

"Have you tried these mashed potatoes?" she said in her sleep. Mashed potatoes are her favorite side dish. Period.

One of my church members puts Velveeta cheese in the mashed potatoes, along with the butter, to get his kids to eat them. It is good. I opted to make them that way, after I went to the grocery store to get some other stuff. I scored a pre-cooked chicken. I have no idea why they are cheaper than raw chicken at the same store, but so be it. Some frozen peas and a little store-bought gravy for the spuds went into the cart, and I was set.

"This is great!" she scooped the mashed potatoes, "Thanks for understanding my decision fatigue."

"That's not a thing," I said.

"You can google it."

"You can also google Bigfoot," I said.

A few days later, we were sitting on the porch. "Whatchy thinking?" she asked.

"Oh, nothing."

"You've been staring into nothing for five minutes."

"Well," I said, "It is going to be warm tomorrow, so the morning hours are going to be the coolest. But, all the retired guys live closer to the beagle clubs and get there real early. So, I am not sure if I should run then or bank on it raining later. The forecast says it should rain in the afternoon, and the rain would allow the afternoon chase to be safe temperatures."

"Oh," she said. "I guess either way."

"Well, it also depends on which club I want to attend. That depends on the order of hospital visits tomorrow. I have people in hospitals close to each club. The question is, how early is too early to visit someone in the hospital. I will probably only run from five to eight if I go in the morning. Is eight o'clock too early? If so, I will probably wait and run in the afternoon rain."

"I guess it depends on the patient."

"True, and I will have to decide what dogs to take. I like taking Duke, but he can't keep up with his pups for very long."

"Maybe you should leave him at home," she said.

"Well," I replied, "I have that one pup that has started running groundhogs. Constantly. Duke is my tattle tale. If it is a groundhog, he won't go along. I can then correct the others."

"I think you have decision fatigue," she smacked her lips as if to tell me that she was vindicated in her views.

"Get outta here."

"So you have made a decision? I don't think you have."

"Absolutely. I will run in the morning, and I will take old Duke along, and we will go to West Branch Beagle Club."

"Oh," she sounded dejected, "I guess I was wrong."

I will be honest; I just said that answer on the spot without thinking it through. I could have blurted out a different answer entirely, but I wanted to be assertive. I couldn't admit that she was right. Cripes, we just started living together.

SOPHISTICATED

My wife is more sophisticated than I am. Granted, this is as obvious as a horsefly on a powdered donut hole to anyone who knows me. You see, my wife, Renee, travels a lot for her work at the university. She has been to Disney more than all of my relatives combined because that is where academic conferences tend to occur. Well, she has also been to Vegas more than a career gambler. Sin City is another popular destination for her work conferences. She is also a big fan of trying new things at our local restaurants too.

"Why don't you try the smoked pig cheeks?" she asked me one time.

"Because," I said, "I don't know if I will like it. I know I like brisket, so I got that."

"Well," she dismissed my hesitance, "You were probably a picky eater as a kid, too. Did you always choose the same thing then?"

"Yeah," I said, "I chose what my mother cooked. The other option was not to eat at all."

That, I suppose, is why I tend not to order things I have never tried while at a restaurant. Going without food as a kid was free. Going without food at a restaurant costs $20 plus tip. Incidentally, I tried pork cheek at a pig roast not long ago, and it was delicious. One night this summer, I trained the hunting beagles until dark and then went home. I fed the dogs, put my Tek 2.0 SportDOG tracking collars on the charging station, and poured a big glass of iced tea.

"What do you want for supper?" Renee asked.

"I am flexible," I said, "It is hot outside, so I am not in the mood to eat much. Maybe another glass of tea will be enough. Something cold."

"How about charcuterie?" she asked.

"What?"

"You like it. Remember, you had it when we were at the restaurant last month."

"I doubt it," I said.

"It was served on a wooden board. There was salami, capicola, brie, feta, and cheddar," Renee counted each item on her fingers as she looked to the ceiling to jar her memory."

"Oh. Well, yeah, why don't you just call it processed meat and cheese."

"Preserved. Not processed. Charcuterie is a variety of processes to preserve meat, and it is intended for you to savor the flavors that are bestowed by curing and smoking."

"Um. Okay. I will eat breadless sandwiches if that is what you are in the mood for," I said, "It can be on a regular plate, too, if we don't have any extra cutting boards lying around."

In another instance, Renee called me when she was on her way to a meeting, "Can you make tapas for us tonight?" she asked.

"If you tell me where to find one," I said.

"No!" she said, "Don't you remember we had tapas together?"

"You mean that tilapia fish?"

"I mean tapas. Small plates meant to be shared."

"Small plates of what?"

"Well," Renee sighed, "It can be whatever you want. We have some chicken leftovers, and some pasta salad, and a few hard-boiled eggs that could be deviled."

"Oh," I said, "Yeah. I can cook some warm-ups."

"What are warm-ups?"

"You sophisticated people call it leftovers."

"Well, yes. Our tapas will be leftovers, but that is not what it means. It is small plates of food intended to be shared."

"So, you mean appetizers?"

"Whatever, can you make it? I will be home at eight o'clock tonight."

"And your warm-up appetizers will be waiting!" I said. She just hung up.

At the beginning of August, I was getting the freezer ready for the upcoming hunting season. I had a couple of rabbits in there, a bit of venison, one pheasant, a grouse, and two doves.

"I am bringing home some company," a text from my wife appeared on my phone. I was running dogs. I ignored the text.

"Can you get supper for everyone?" she texted again.

"I guess," I typed back.

"Whatever you want to make is fine. Or buy something. Four people are coming."

"No problem."

"7 pm," she typed. I picked up the dogs and went home.

I made rabbit bratwurst, venison jerky, and noodle soup with all the game birds. I also made these peppers that I stuffed with ground venison that I cooked and then wrapped those same Hungarian wax peppers with crescent rolls. I baked them until they were done. The freezer was now ready for the fall hunting season.

"Wow," Renee said as she entered the house and smelled the food, "Where did you get delivery from?"

"I cooked," was my reply as I handed everyone a saucer. "This here meal is tapas, with a little bit of charcuterie in the form of venison Jerky—perfectly preserved."

"What?" my wife looked nervous.

"I have rabbit bratwurst too, as well as some venison stuffed peppers and a chicken noodle soup made with pheasant, grouse, and dove instead of chicken."

"I have never tried rabbit," one guest said.

"Well," I replied, "It is free to you, which is the best way to try something new."

"This is good!" one guy said.

"Feel free to refill that little plate that goes with the coffee cup," I motioned toward the food, "My wife says that tapas is served on small plates."

"I like this bratwurst a lot," he answered, "Maybe you can teach me to hunt."

"Well, I suppose."

"What do I need?"

"Hmm," I said, "I can loan you a shotgun. Get a pair of brush pants, boots, a hunting vest, an orange hat, and take a hunter's safety course." Who would have thought that these sophisticated types would become hunters because of the desire to try new food? Supper tables are the future for converting people to our sport. Well, my wife calls it dinner, but you know what I mean. It is supper.

BEAGLE YOGA

I was recently in a hospital waiting room, which is an interesting place to study human behavior. Let's face it: no one is there because they are having a great day. You go there for health concerns. Frequently, I will travel to do a hospital visit, and the parishioner that I intend to see is having an MRI, a CAT scan, or some other test. So, I wait in the lobby rather than not see the person after traveling all that way. Sometimes it can take a while. I try to ignore the television, which is often on a channel that features reality TV or some other divisive thing. People will offer live commentary on the program on the television. I think they do this as a way to reach out to others. It can be a full waiting room, and each person is utterly alone as they wait for the doctor to come out with news about their loved one.

"Who in their right mind would do that?" someone will say.

"How about it?" another will answer. Boom, strangers become friends, or at least social with one another and can fill the time with small talk that temporarily relieves the mind from a downward spiral that is destined to contemplate the worst-case scenario. I try to help people in the waiting room in this fashion. On that particular day, I picked up a copy of *State College Magazine* and browsed the contents. State College is home to The Penn State University (they insist that you capitalize The), and the town is an interesting mix of academics and what I call regular people. There was an article on goat yoga.

Now, I am no yoga expert by any means. I was challenged to try it once, and it was a series of poses that were held for a length of time. Eventually, they get difficult to hold because although you aren't lifting weights, there is a limit to how long you can hold your body parts in a position. Remember raising your hand in school, and they would count the hands, and eventually, your arm got tired? Perhaps you have had to do the "dead cockroach" as a punishment on a sports team, where you lay on your back and hold your arms and legs in the air. I don't know how long this punishment is supposed to last, but coaches tend to keep you in that position until all four of your limbs quiver, turn to Jell-O, and collapse to the ground. Then they make you do push-ups.

So, a yoga expert I am not, but I know that the exercises can be difficult, and like any exercise, you feel relaxed at the end. This article, however, mentioned some summer activities that the State College resident might want to do, and one was a trip to Carlisle, Pennsylvania, where you can do yoga with ten miniature goats running around you. The article quoted an expert on Goat yoga, and she said that it is just like regular yoga, except you might have a goat sneeze in your face or poop on your mat. Get this, you only have to pay $35 to have an hour of goat mucus in your face and turds under your body. So, that sounds like a real deal there. That one-hour experience is limited to a class of 30. The article didn't say why the class was limited to 30, but I would presume that each goat probably has a limit of snot and poo. 30 would make a three-to-one goat ratio, and that probably ensures that each person gets to really smell a goat and get their full $35 worth of goat yoga. The owner makes $1,050.00 in that hour, which is a good wage.

I only know a few people who do yoga regularly, and both are prone to go on an all-juice diet at times. They will make juice out of any combination of things, often vegetables. I tried the juice once when a gal who works with my wife, Renee, stopped by at supper time. We were having a cookout, but she was a vegan and brought her food. The juice was part of a cleanse. She was kind of an evangelist for veganism and brought samples for everyone to try. Have you ever drunk V-8 Juice? This stuff was nothing like that.

"How is it?" She asked me.

"What is it supposed to taste like?" I asked.

"What do you taste?"

"Garlic," I said.

"Yeah, that helps the taste a lot," she said, "It is cabbage, celery, lettuce, and spinach."

"Those things all taste good," I said.

"But it can be kinda tasteless once you remove the pulp. You get mostly water on the other side. I had an onion-infused version for lunch."

"Good thing you and my wife do a lot of work online; with all the garlic and onions, you might really stink up a room," I said.

"What?" she looked perturbed.

"Not me," I said, "I love garlic. But it can be hard when I visit people. I used to eat raw leeks as a kid. They grew up right next to the school. They taste like a mixture of onions and garlic. At recess, we would go the woods line, eat some, and get sent home from school for smelling bad."

"I have had leeks from the store, and they do not taste like that."

"These leeks I am talking ablut grow in the wild, in the spring, and are sometimes called ramps," I explained.

"I need some of those for my juice."

"I will give you some next year."

"Can I go with you?"

"I don't know. I try not to share the spots where they grow. If they are over-harvested, they will not grow back. People who use them as a side dish will often pick too many. Why, you are basically planning to live on liquefied leeks for a month. I will get you a good batch. Nothing personal." Needless to say, she took it personally.

Renee knows another yoga enthusiast who is not a vegan. She will eat eggs and, at times, fish. She will occasionally eat chicken, the way that some people will occasionally eat a steak. Her name is Sue.

"You do the juice cleanses?" I asked her.

"No," she said, "I prefer salads and utilize a coffee cleanse."

"I hear ya." I said, "Coffee has that effect on me too."

"You don't understand," Sue said.

"I do, too," I said, "It isn't a polite topic for adults to discuss, but a lot of people have to go do number two after having coffee."

"It is a coffee colonic cleanse," she said.

"Pardon me?"

"It is a coffee cleanse utilizing an enema," she said. I was speechless. "What are you thinking?" she asked me.

"I am guessing you have to let the coffee cool off first," I said, and that was the end of the conversation.

But I got to thinking about it, and I could probably start a Beagle Yoga. I wouldn't be as greedy; I would only charge $20 per person. However, anyone who knows a beagle knows that they can easily give attention to five people at least. So, my class would still have 30 students. They would set their mats on the ground inside my fenced yard. Next, I would pulverize four bags of the Snausage dog treats. My dogs love those. I would then scatter the Snausage dust all around the yoga mats. That is going to guarantee some face-to-face time with a beagle. Heck, it might even ensure some massive tail wags against your face if you are in one of those positions where your head is on the ground.

The overexcitement from the favorite treat would no doubt induce some reverse sneezing that beagles are known for. The reverse sneeze would be just as amazing as the goats' forward sneeze, but you would not get your face wet. While I doubt that the beagles would poop on a mat, I can obviously just not clean the yard on the day before the class. This might ensure that a couple of random yogis would put their mats on top of some processed Purina.

The goat yoga website also mentioned that they have a goat yoga/wine-tasting event as well. That involves hauling the goats to a winery, and they can combine goat yoga and wine. It costs $50 each. Again, I think I can come in at a better price. For $40, I will take you to the woods and you get to listen to the beagles chase rabbits. The sound of hounds chasing would be the elevated version, better than watching them eat snacks. The $40 is a steal because everyone knows that I will be there for more than an hour. We will do this yoga class at dawn. When we get done running dogs, I will have coffee for everyone. Use it however you want . . .

EXCUSES

Ah, the month of May always makes me think of Mother's Day. Looking back, I can see that my mother was a saint. She had to be in order to deal with my nonsense. I wouldn't say that I was a bad kid, but neither was Dennis the Menace. Things just always seemed to happen. By the time I became a teenager, my life had gone to the dogs, literally, and all I wanted to do was be in the woods with the dogs during the day and hang out with my friends in the evening. In fact, I had become an expert at ditching school.

Don't get me wrong, I planned the ditching well. I made sure that there were no tests or quizzes that I would miss. Also, I made sure that I was marked as present so that I did not get an absence put on my report card. I had no problem cutting class, but I drew the line at having to forgery. If I were absent, then I would have to produce a written excuse the next day and present it to the nurse to explain why I was missing the day before. I could not take the chance of writing a not from Mom. The key to getting away while being marked as attending was to go to homeroom. At homeroom, the teacher took attendance. That teacher then noted all the absences and a student would run the list of absent kids to the office. The secretary would then compile a master list of all the absent kids from the entire school, and that list would then be duplicated on a mimeograph machine. The names all fit on one sheet of paper. These duplicates were made by applying ink to the page, and they were a bit damp when freshly made. They had a distinct odor to them, which makes me think of quizzes and exams because many teachers did not have the tests duplicated until right before class. At any rate, an administrative assistant would slide the list of sick kids under every classroom during the first period. It would suddenly slide across the waxed floor. Most teachers never looked at it. In other words, attendance was only taken once.

I often volunteered to take the list of absentee students from my homeroom to the office secretary. This is because you would then be near the office when the bell rang to end homeroom and send you to the first period. I would duck into the bathroom and wait for the bell that indicated the start of the first period to ring. Then, I bolted out a side door and into the woods. I would then walk home, the teachers having tabulated me as presently at school, and plan my day. I would sneak into the backyard of my house, leash my two beagles, and head afield. A half mile from my house was a spot where I could run. A couple hundred yards away was a tangled mass of weeds and goldenrod that held cottontails in abundance. If I went behind the baseball field, I could run cottontails and catch trout in the river. The day was full of possibilities. I just had to make sure that my mother did not see me returning home from school and grabbing the dogs. I kept a fishing pole in the kennel with my fishing vest.

One of my favorite times to ditch class was at the end of the school year, often in May. That is when we had "assemblies." Assemblies were when the entire school would gather in the Auditorium for an enriching program. Often, they consumed the entire afternoon. There was at least one per week in May, often on a Friday. There was always a slide show presented by the Photography Club that showed the entire year in review. Student Council always had a presentation that was intended to help teenagers transition from childhood to adulthood. It had lots of contemporary music and positive messages on the video screen that basically explained that angst is normal and you should explore your emotions.

A motivational speaker was often brought into the school to inspire students to dream big. Once, they brought in a guy to scare kids from doing drugs. It was the Actor from the television show Baretta. Remember that show? It was about an undercover cop with a giant white bird on his shoulder. Anyway, in the 1980s, he was no longer playing that character and instead was touring schools and speaking about the horrors of drugs. I don't remember the programming for other assemblies because I was obviously not there. I mastered the science of playing hooky and then turned it into an art form. It didn't hurt that I did pretty well in my classes, and I was the last kid that my teachers would expect to do this. I just had to be judicious in how often I pulled this stunt.

Assemblies were perfect skip days. Most students liked assemblies. They would be sure to attend those days. I am sure the assemblies were also a time for the teachers to get a rest, especially at the end of the school year. Back then, teachers calculated grades by hand, and you could almost guarantee that there was nothing in the last week, or even the last two weeks, that would be graded. You were issued your final report card on the last day of class. I am talking about hand-written report cards that had to be produced by each teacher filling out your card. The last two weeks of the academic year were the equivalent of the garbage time at the end of a sporting event, where the outcome is already determined, and you are just running out the clock. Only the teachers were frantically crunching numbers to get the report cards done. By the time I graduated in 1990, some teachers had started using computers to make their grade books easy and self-calculating, but not all of them were tech-savvy. And the ones that did have computers calculate the grades, still had to get a pen to fill out the report card.

Well, it came to pass that I got caught in my senior year. Students returned to homeroom before going to an assembly, and my homeroom teacher noticed that I had been present for homeroom but not for the gathering before the assembly.

The phone rang after supper. "Hello?" I answered.

"Bob?" my homeroom teacher asked.

"Yes."

"Mr. Herring here. I am sure I saw you this morning. But you were gone after lunch. Let me talk to your parents." I covered the part of the phone that you talk into. This was back when people had landlines, and you could actually hear what was said.

"Mom," I said, "It's one of my teachers. He wants to talk to you. Just so you know, I went to school and left so that I could go fishing and run dogs. I'm basically in big trouble. But I didn't want to watch a slide show for two hours." She looked at me with disbelief.

"Hello?" my Mom said. There was a pause. I couldn't hear the other side.

"I wasn't here this afternoon if you called," she said. She kept nodding her head.

"Well," she said, "Of course, he wasn't there after lunch. He was with me today. I took him to the dentist." Now I got nervous. The list of absentee kids also listed all the permissible early dismissals for things like a doctor's appointment. You had to take a note from your parents to the nurse before homeroom for that. But then you could just walk out the door and wait for your Mom to pick you up. No escort, no fuss.

"I see," Mom said, "Not on the list? Hmm. Could you hold on?"

She pulled the phone away from her head, but barely, and yelled, "What did you do with the excuse I gave you!?" I looked dumbfounded at her and started to answer, but she put her finger to her nose to silence me."

My mother then spoke into the phone, "The absent-minded brat still has it in his pocket. You want me to punish him, or you? We both can if you want." Another pause. "Okay, thanks for following up."

She hung up and hurriedly wrote on a sheet of paper, "Take this excuse to school with you tomorrow. It is dated for today."

"Umm. Thanks," I was bewildered. "Why did you do that?"

"I don't know. You aren't usually too much trouble. At least not like this." She sipped her coffee.

"You going to tell Dad?" I asked.

"Yeah, I will. On his day off from work. He won't care if I tell him then."

"There is an assembly on Thursday," I said, "Can I just skip the whole day? Get an excuse written by you for that?"

Much to my surprise, Mom went to the calendar and came back to me, "Sure, you can do that." Now, I was starting to think that she had undergone some sort of personality change. But I was elated. I was awake before dawn when Thursday rolled around. I grabbed my boots and dog leashes.

"I think I will run hare today!" I said.

"I don't think so," Mom answered.

"Why not?"

"You'll be busy all day."

"Doing what?"

"Driving your grandmother."

"Where?"

"Monday is Memorial Day," she pointed a finger at me and made a clicking sound with her tongue. I instantly knew what was happening.

"Okay," I said. My grandmother planted flowers at almost a dozen cemeteries in advance of Memorial Day for Veterans as well as every other relative. Generations of aunts, uncles, and distant cousins. This was a good thing to do. However, the day would also be filled with her trying to remember where certain graves were, lengthy deliberations about what flowers should go on what grave and taking two and three attempts to find tiny cemeteries that were down dirt roads that seemed to lead to nowhere. We would have to stop and eat somewhere. We would visit some of her friends. I wouldn't be done until after supper. Gram would, of course, bombard me with questions about what

I was going to do for a living and lecture me about the dangers in life.

"You didn't think you were going to go without being punished for skipping school, did you?" Mom asked.

"I guess not," I smiled. It was still better than an assembly. And one of those remote cemeteries had an access road where both sides had been logged since I was last there. I wouldn't have seen how good of a rabbit hunting spot it really was had I not driven there.

LANDLINES WITHOUT ID

The fact that telemarketers can now bombard my cell phone while pretending to be from a local town is frustrating. In part, this is because I am a field trial secretary, and I never know when I will get a phone call from someone trying to get info about our club's trial. The magazine advertising lists my phone number.

"Hello," I answered a couple weeks ago.

"From what I can see in this advertisement, your club is having a trial on April 6 and 7."

"Yes, sir."

"It says males on Sunday instead of Saturday."

"Correct. Lycoming Beagle Club is close by. We have it set up so that you could run both trials."

"I see," he said, "And the ad says you are at 145 Beagle Club Road. Lock Haven."

"We are," I answered.

"So what would I type into my GPS?"

"Just what you said."

"So, I just type the 145 Beagle Club Road, Lock Haven, Pennsylvania."

"That's right. Or take the Woolrich exit off of I99 and follow the wooden signs like we used to do."

"I want no part of that."

I was born back in the 1900s and have been trained differently. Let me explain. First of all, I remember when a phone call was mysterious. Back then, the phone was a massive box that hung on your kitchen wall. When it rang, you had no idea who it was. Nowadays, my wife, Renee, looks up at the television screen and can tell exactly who is calling.

"That's my friend Kate," she said once, "She called me four times today. I will call her back later." Renee kept right on matching socks in the laundry basket and never even looked for the phone. That is another big difference. Landlines were anchored to the wall. We have a landline, but it is a system that includes three cordless phones. If you did want to answer the phone, it might be problematic because none of the phones are in their charging cradles, one of them has probably been AWOL long enough that it has a dead battery, and the other two could be anyplace ranging from the top of the refrigerator to stuffed in between the couch cushions.

When I was a kid, there was no way to know who was calling. Caller I.D. had not yet arrived. So, there was almost excitement. Who could it be? Maybe someone is calling to do something! When our landline rings now, no one reacts. Other than to look at the caller I.D. if the television is on. As a kid, it was a mad dash to get to the phone. My sister and I both responded, hoping that it was some great opportunity to play a game, go fishing, or something.

Then again, the phone didn't ring that much. Not like it does now, and I guess that is because of the contemporary abundance of telemarketers. Back in the 1900s, the phone might not ring for hours at a time. Today, even when you do answer the call, you may find that the machine that dialed your number has hung up because you haven't answered fast enough. Then it rings again in two minutes. And repeat. My latest batch of calls has been from people wanting me to change the company that sends me the electric bill. They all read a script. An identical script tells me that I have the right to change. No matter which company calls, the script they read is the same. I always wait for them to finish.

"You did very well," I recently said to one such call.

"What?" he asked.

"Reading. You read that script very well. Much better than the person that read it to me yesterday."

"Who called you yesterday?"

"I don't know," I answered, "But he mispronounced a lot of words. You said 'electric' perfectly. The guy yesterday said 'eletric.' Granted, that is a common pronunciation of the word, but I am sure it isn't written that way on your script."

"So," he continued, "Can I sign you up?"

"Nah," I said. "I just told you I got the same script yesterday. You only offer the cheaper rate briefly, then the rate skyrockets."

"Why would you say that, Sir?"

"Because I know this is a scam to prey upon the elderly. If they don't catch every piece of mail you send them, they go from saving a few bucks per month to losing hundreds of dollars each month."

"What is your reason for saying that?"

"I am a pastor, and when some poor old guy or widow on a fixed income gets an exorbitant electric bill, they sometimes call the church.'

"We don't do that."

"Did you call your grandparents or aging relatives to offer this fantastic deal to them?"

Click. The other end went blank. And if it isn't a call about electric bills, it is a credit card plan, medicine for back pain, or some other scam.

Now, I have the dang phone in my pocket. Instead of being on the wall at home, it is always with me. No matter where I go. I do leave the phone in my truck when I am in church or doing hospital and nursing home visits.

"Why don't you take your phone with you?" Renee asked me.

"Because," I said, "If someone is recovering from surgery, or heaven forbid dying, I do not want to tell them that they have to wait a minute while my wife tells me what groceries to get on the way home." The phone can sit in the truck, untouched, for a few hours.

All this brings me to a day a few weeks ago when I arrived at the beagle club with four dogs, all wearing GPS collars. I turned on the collars and cut them loose. Then I realized I had left the handheld at home. I couldn't track them if I wanted. I had a brief moment of anxiety. Then I thought, "Hey. I drove an hour to get here. I am not going to pick them up and go home."

Sometimes, when the rabbits are coming quickly and the chases are good, I can go for an entire rabbit hunt without looking at the handheld. And that is in hunting season. Here, I was inside the fence with rabbits everywhere. They locked onto a bunny, and the chase was on. After a bit, it started to rain, and I sat under the pavilion at the club. The rain pounded on the tin roof, but I could still faintly hear the dogs across the small creek and up the hill, driving the rabbit in the high scent. When it was time to go, I caught up to them and leashed them. It was just like the 1980s when I first started with beagles.

"I forgot my handheld," I said to Renee at dinner.

"Oh," she said, "How did that go?"

"It was fine," I shrugged my shoulders.

"Oh," Renee stabbed some potatoes, "So you won't be trying to hog outlets to ever charge collars again?"

"I will not," I said, "I will only hog the outlets in my office, and that reminds me, I have to charge collars." Hey, I don't want to be a slave to technology, but it is pretty handy. After all, the whole time I ran those dogs, I knew that I could call Renee to drive that handheld to me if I got in trouble. She never leaves her phone in the car, like I do. I guess I want the good old days and the technology, too.

Spring-ish Cleaning

When the weather warms, we will find ourselves in full-blown spring cleaning. This is typified by the opening of windows, the cleaning of windows, the gusts of fresh wind through the halls of our home, and the scrubbing. But we are still in March, and that means that we are in the midst of spring-like or spring-ish cleaning. What does that mean in my house?

March 1st is the first day of the running season here in Pennsylvania. In terms of the beagling life, I only have two seasons. Running season and gunning season. Running season goes from March 1st until mid-October. Then, it is hunting season until the last day of February. Spring-ish cleaning begins with the transfer of some things out of my truck. Firstly is the orange. Our hunting laws require the use of fluorescent orange, and I own a vest, a few shirts, quite a few hats, and even a couple of headbands that can make a non-orange hat legal. The orange lives as a blob in the back seat of my truck from October until March, and different weather calls for a different orange. The blob undulates throughout the season as warmer coats, rain gear, and wool pullovers are added to the blob, as the weather dictates. Oh, a pair of bib coveralls or two also join the blob. The coveralls are important for afternoon hunts during the hunting season.

I learned a long time ago that it was good to hunt for an hour every day. As a pastor my parish is fine with this practice. They realize that I have work during the morning and afternoon that consists of hospital visits and clergy gatherings. Meetings are typically at night because most church members who serve on committees have a job. I tend to hunt in the last hour of daylight because it is good to know your limitations. The Bible says that

Jesus was tempted for forty days and forty nights in the desert and was offered about anything a person could have wanted. He, of course, resisted, but there have been plenty of days when I have succumbed to good hunting conditions.

"Hello?" I answered my phone years ago.

"Where are you?" my wife, Renee, asked.

"Trying to kill a rabbit," I said. "I shot two already, and this one is really sneaky."

"You know that it is nine o'clock in the morning, right?"

"Really?"

"Yeah," she sighed, "You were supposed to unlock the church for the pastors' prayer group. Did you forget about the meeting?"

"Can you unlock it?" I asked, "I will catch the dogs and get there right away. Wait, they are circling back; I will just wait here. I gotta go; this call is making too much noise…"

So, during workdays, I don't drop the tailgate until the last hour of daylight. I throw the bibs over the Dockers to protect them, put on some boots, and hit the briars. I can only hunt for an hour because it gets dark. It eliminates my temptation to hunt until mid-morning. I might if I start at dawn. It pays to know your weaknesses. Anyway, the coveralls add a certain critical density to the blob. The end result is that there are many days in the hunting season when I can only find one orange hat despite having three or four in there. At spring-ish cleaning, when I unload all the hunting clothes, I am amazed at how much is in the truck. I just keep taking more and more out of the cab, like those endless handkerchiefs that magicians pull out of a pocket. My backseat is like Oscar the Grouch's garbage can. No matter how much you take out, more emerges.

All of that stuff gets moved into the house. I used to move it 10 feet into the house. Then, the blob coagulates and begins to churn again. It stayed there for a few days until I was able to get the burdock and beggar's lice removed. I simply take the garments outside, one at a time, and scrape the unwanted material off the clothes with the dull end of a knife. If it took more than a few days, I ended up in marital court. A marital court is different than a court-martial insofar as a court-martial has orderly proceedings and a legal defense. Marital court is my wife laying down the law. It isn't a fair process.

"You got all those clothes put away?" Renee said one year.

"Not yet," I replied, "Didn't you see some of them are still in the entryway?"

"I did," she glared at me, "When did you plan on finishing that job."

"Soon."

"I hope so. Tomorrow, I am putting it in garbage bags and throwing it out." That is marital court. And she meant it. So, I now put them in the downstairs bathroom, in this small shower that no one wants to use because the geniuses who built our house put the bathroom between the kitchen and the living room. Not very close to the clothes in the upstairs bedroom. It never gets used. She doesn't even look in there.

At spring-ish cleaning, I also bring in a plastic bin of ammo that lives on the passenger side floor of my truck for all of rabbit season. I use four different shotguns. In part, this is because I will take a 16 when I expect to encounter pheasants or a 20-gauge if grouse are abundant or a flight of woodcock are passing through. I think .410 is my current favorite. Each day, from October until February, I may unload the ammo loops in my vest, removing one gauge of shells and replacing them with another. The full cardboard box of shotgun shells is as durable a shipping container as you can imagine. Once you open it and remove just one shell, it becomes the most fragile packaging in modern commerce. It falls apart. So, as that happens, I put the shells into a plastic bin with a lid. .410, 20 gauge, 16, it all mixes. It is like the clothes blob but more contained. Spring-ish cleaning involves bringing this ammo into the house and sorting it so that I can take inventory and look for what is on sale in the wake of the end of hunting season.

It is also at this time of year that my wife goes through some late winter cleaning. She gets a little cabin fever and isn't really interested in walking around the woods with me and the beagles while the hard snow is on the ground. There are a few things that she will typically do to brighten her mood in March. One is towels. Not the kind you actually use, but the decorative ones that you hang on the handles of cabinets or towel racks in bathrooms. Woe be to you if you use one of these decorations to dry your hands, especially if you have just cleaned rabbits, even if you rinse your hands very well before you dry them.

This year, Renee put new lightbulbs in the bathroom above the glass medicine cabinet. Five glass bulbs are there, and they illuminate the bathroom. I am not sure where she got the new ones, but I walked into the bathroom to shower at four o'clock in the morning, and the lights were blazing. I mean, it reminds you of those old movies where they interrogate the bad guy under the bright light. But these things are even brighter. Each one of these five bulbs is more than we need to illuminate the bathroom.

I was at a field trial one time, and somebody suddenly flipped on one of those bright LED light bars that adorn the entire roof of many pickup trucks these days. I was standing in front of the truck, and the sudden shift from darkness to blinding light was startling. My bathroom is like that now. Except it is like having five of those light bars, come on at once. Sheesh. I showered in the dark; I figured I would be fine. But my wife has a perimeter of hair goop, hair helper, hair volumizer, and hair conditioner running all three walls of our tub/shower. The only wall not lined with these items is the curtain. There is also moisturizer and soap for oily skin, soap for dry skin, a shower cap in case she doesn't have time to let her hair drip dry, bubble bath, and wash rags. I kid you not; one of those wash clothes is decorative. It just hangs there in the shower. At any rate, she can walk under all these hanging, stainless steel baskets that are suspended from torsion bar rods. They hit me on the chin if I walked into them, and that is just what I did, all because I was trying to avoid new light bulbs. One of the containers must not have been closed all the way, and when the basket crashed into the shower floor and landed on my foot, it began to leak. Hopping on one foot in a wet shower is dangerous under ideal circumstances, let alone when the floor of the tub has been greased with hair moisturizer.

My landing was loud enough to wake Renee, and she yelled from the bedroom, which was just across the hall.

"Are you okay?" She yelled.

"I think so."

"What happened?!"

"I fell!"

"Did you get hurt?!"

"I don't think so!"

"Get cut?!"

"I don't know!"

"Why not?!"

"There is no light in here!"

"I just put new light bulbs in there! There should be plenty of light!"

"Okay!"

"Speaking of showers, I noticed that you put all your hunting clothes in the downstairs shower. I decided to store the old hand towels in there until winter. You better get them moved before I throw them out."

Marital court strikes again.

HEARING LOSS & SNOW

February, in recent years, has become our snowy month. The weatherman says that this is due to the fact that in recent years, Lake Erie does not freeze like it typically does. So, when the winds howl out of the northwest, they are able to collect moisture from the unfrozen lake surface and then deposit it in Pennsylvania. I, for one, like February snow for a couple of reasons. One is that it lets me see rabbits easily. There seems to be a stigma with shooting white hares on brown ground, but we routinely shoot brown cottontails in the winter. I spent much of the early season hearing cottontails run through cover so thick I could not see them. If conversations with my wife, Renee, are any indicator, these rabbits must be close because my hearing is not what it used to be.

"Could you take care of the garage?" she asked me a few weeks ago.

"Sure," I said, "Right after this coffee."

"Okay, I am going to work."

I went out to the garage, took a broom to the leaves that entered while butchering a deer, and moved the old dog box that was in the way. We have one of those garages that are so full of stuff that no car ever goes inside of it. I arranged the boxes and got everything situated so that it could be accessed. The entire process took 2 hours. I then took a shower and went to work.

"You lied to me over coffee this morning," Renee greeted me at the door.

"What?"

"I asked you to do something, and you said you would."

"I did do it!" I defended myself, "And it isn't perfect, but I put over two hours into it, and it looks a lot better than it did!"

"Two hours? What did you do? It's still there!" She pointed her hand across the kitchen.

"Of course, it is still there," I said, "When you told me to take care of it, did you mean that I should get rid of it?"

"Well," she sighed, "Obviously!" Again, she pointed across the kitchen.

"It's part of the foundation of the house, honey," I explained, "We can't get rid of it. We can remodel it, but it is part of the basement."

"Garbage is not holding our house up," she looked at me like I was crazy.

"Some of those boxes could be thrown out, but the garage itself has to stay."

"What are you talking about?" she said.

"You told me to take care of the garage. It got dirty in deer season."

"I told you to take care of the garbage. Today was garbage day." She pointed across the kitchen again at the garbage can.

"Well, stop yelling at me," I said, "Because that would have been a lot easier than what I did."

What I am saying is that if I could hear those running rabbits, they had to be close. Snow makes the whole hunting process a lot easier. I like the winter hunting season a lot.

The other thing I like about snow is that it is the best time of year to find new hunting spots. I lose good hunting spots all the time. I have lost them to strip mines, parking lots, housing developments, shopping malls, and overhunting. I live in a part of the world where lots of guys hunt—at least deer and maybe turkey. I am probably the most passionate rabbit hunter where I live. I have a truck with a rooftop tent for camping while running dogs, and I have a dog box in the pack. It is pretty easy to notice. On several trips afield last year, I was followed by the same vehicle everywhere I went. Sure enough, that guy has a beagle that sits on a chain for ten months per year, and he wants it to run like a champion for the eight weekends he wants to hunt. He found a few of my spots, and he jump shoots rabbits in front of his pudgy beagle because it isn't able to circle a rabbit.

If you think that is bad, I have known guys who have driven around with their GPS, looking to locate another hunter and then determine where the hunting spot is located. Even worse, I have taken friends to one of my spots only to discover that they are hunting it without me—and they drove hours to get there!

I like snow for locating new hunting spots. I take a dog that I know will not run trash and go looking for rabbit tracks and new honey holes. February is the end of the season anyway, and it is always nice to stumble upon a great new patch of bunny brush. It is always a little exciting to see new places and learn the routes that the local rabbits run.

Winter has changed. The schools tend to cancel over very little snow. I haven't seen a snow shovel worth owning in decades. They are all plastic and unable to chop ice. I break two per year.

To make matters worse, the coal mines are now all surface mined, and it is almost impossible to find a good coal shovel to do a thorough shoveling. I saw one for sale in an Antique store for over $100. So, I keep busting the cheap shovels.

I do not get to wear snowshoes very often here in Pennsylvania, but even the new synthetic shoes are different than the traditional ones. I like getting into the snow drifts and looking for the story in the snow that tells me what has been going on at night when I was away.

Heck, kids don't even stand at bus stops. The driver stops at each house and gets the kid from inside the warm house or idling car. They don't even have to stand in a windy bus stop and keep warm by outrunning bullies. Bullies were an important part of childhood, especially at the bus stop. The bus stop is where you were unable to avoid the bully. You couldn't run too far because you had to be there when the bus came. It was better to take a punch from a bully than to go home and say that you missed the bus. Also, it was better to tell the bus driver that you were running to the bus stop because you left the house late than to say that you were avoiding a bully.

There is no bus stop anymore, and I am late all the time because the only thing that stops more than a school bus is some of my hunting companions to pee! I know that I sound like a grumpy old man, and I feel bad about that. Some things have not changed. I love fresh snow and the chance to find tracks. I still love wool clothes better than any modern material, even Thinsulate. All the scientists and engineers have yet to improve on the wool that God gave a sheep. So, whenever the world panics at a snowstorm, and schools cancel, I take a solidarity day with the kids. I skip work and go to the brush and look for that marvelous Moment when a beagle sticks his nose into the snow, and a rabbit that is covered with snow and no visible tracks leading to it emerges in a burst of energy to run out into the pine trees with a beagle or two or four in pursuit. The hounds have to calm down after they lose sight of him, and then they start to chase with their noses.

It is a joyous thing when they call for an accumulating snow. The local news has a new gal that gives the weather in the morning. As far as I can tell, she knows very little about meteorology. She mostly reads the numbers that are already on the screen behind her. So, I rely on the rumor mill to tell me when it is going to snow. I get phone calls. "Pastor, are we having Bible study tonight? It's going to snow." Then, the mad dash for milk and bread (and toilet paper) begins, and I get excited at the possibility of going into the deep woods to look for rabbits in a spot I have never hunted. I think they are calling for such a snowstorm tonight, and I want to go hunting tomorrow.

If you will excuse me, I have to talk to my wife. She just gave me an order from the other room while I was typing this story. I would tell you what I think she said, but it can't be right. I want to make sure that I have time to hunt tomorrow. That poor hearing that resulted in cleaning the garage might result in a chore that will take way more time than I want to waste on a morning with a good pile of fresh powder for the dogs to hunt. I hope you all enjoy your February. Oh, and as a Pennsylvania native, never trust what a groundhog says about the winter.

COVERTLY

Like you, I am a hound guy. And we know what that means. Now, I am not a man who gets too far into the idea of maligning other hunters. I know an archery friend who gets as mad as can be when he sees a picture of a deer with a crossbow. He says it is unfair, but at the same time, he is pulling a compound bow with pulleys, and when he gets to full draw, the weight lets off, and he is looking through a peepsight! Then you talk to the crowd that hunts traditional archery, and they think the compound bow is cheating because it too uses too much technology, and they will refer to those pulleys as training wheels—like what a kid puts on a bicycle to learn how to ride. Meanwhile, the guy using the traditional longbow or recurve is also using state-of-the-art fiberglass as one of the layers in the bow, and in the case of bows that have removable limbs, they utilize case-hardened bolts, which are also quite modern technology. Oh, it is fun to listen to them argue with each other, but I can't help but think that we would do better to be in favor of all sorts of hunting.

Oh, being hound hunters, we face the wrath of lots of fellow outdoorsmen. In archery season, the guys on state game lands will often get very upset at me if I drop a pack of rabbit dogs on the same state game lands. They often think that it will force deer out of the area, but my beagles are not deer dogs and will not chase deer. Some archers actually do realize this, and love to get set up before I arrive, and once the hounds start circling bunnies, the deer will get up from their beds and walk past the hunter in his tree stand. It is like a deer drive, but the deer aren't on a full sprint.

Those who have deer dogs get into conflict with the deer hunters, too, and despite the fact that both are hunting deer, the conflict between them can be greater than the tensions amongst archery hunters, just because of a different methodology—using dogs versus still hunting. Me? Do I get upset with other hunters? No, but sometimes I pick on the bird hunters.

"What are you wearing around your neck?" I asked a friend one day.

"That's a flush counter. As a rabbit hunter, you have probably never seen one before."

"I got news for you," I said, "I have seen a bunch of them. My grandmother called them stitch counters, and she used them while knitting. In addition to the stitch counters, I tease them about the whole wardrobe fiasco. Hanging out with a bird hunter can make you think that you are at a fashion contest of some sort. Those guys can even walk like models on a catwalk so that you can see their socks with the tassels and the "upland" pants that they think are briar-proof, but as a guy who gets into the thick cover with some regularity, I would classify these pants more as "briar resistant" but only against the mild vegetation—like stinging nettles. When those things are introduced to multi-floral rose or green briar, well, the material may as well be silk.

Of course, they scoff at me and my bibs. "Do you always wear bibs when you hunt?" My friend, Tom Keer, asked when he was visiting to write a rabbit hunting article for Outdoor Life.

"Yes."

"And why is that?" Tom asked, adjusting the flush counter around his neck.

"Vines that wrap around my legs can't pull at my pants, and then I do not have to keep pulling them up. Also, there are lots of good bib coveralls out there that are fantastic at stopping briars.

"Tell him the truth about why you wear bibs," my wife, Renee, snarked.

"What?" I asked.

"My husband has no butt. Flat as a board. He can't keep his pants up!" She laughed and got quite a giggle over that.

And the bird guys have their own language. They don't have hunting spots; they have coverts. Sometimes they do not pronounce the t, and pronounce it as a cover rather than a covert. This terminology is actually one that I now use, too, because of the one hunter type that can make me upset. The type that has no respect for policies, customs, and accepted practices. Some conventions do not have to be written rules; there is just a code. For instance, if you borrowed my truck, it would not have to be said that you should not return it to me with the fuel gauge on empty. In fact, the commonly accepted convention is that you would return it with more fuel than it had, probably even full. No one says this policy out loud, but we all know it. However, we all have that friend or relative who uses the truck to get something and then drifts the vehicle back into the driveway on fumes. I have already had to pour the lawnmower gas into my truck tank to have enough fuel to make it to the gas station! This is an unspoken code and one that we all follow.

And in the world of hunting, here is another big code: If you take me to a great spot, I will not go back there unless you are with me and invite me, even if the landowner would let me hunt it. My friend Mike has a spot with so many rabbits that we always get our limit when we go there. It isn't far from his hunting camp, but I live a half hour away, whereas his home is closer to two hours away; it is an Amish farm, and he asked the farmer for permission, and if you know the Amish, you know that they are very accepting of hunters and will usually be quite cooperative, especially when it comes to removing rabbits from a farm. I know the farmer would let me hunt there, but I would never do that. The same holds when someone goes with me to a spot. What has happened now is this—guys follow me to steal my spots. Can you imagine? Hey, my truck sticks out like a sore thumb, and everyone knows that in my little corner of the world, I am the rabbit guy; this is where I use the bird-dog language. My hunting spots are all coverts because I have to enter covertly! It is like espionage. One hunter follows in a four-wheel drive with very little ground clearance. One day, I led him down an old road that meandered to what was once an old strip mine for coal. I sped ahead to get to a deep rut, which can only be crossed by crossing at an angle almost parallel to the rut itself. I got across and moved ahead. I had trouble crossing, so I knew the little Geo Tracker was going to have difficulty. I went on to my spot—I mean covert—which was nowhere near that location. When I returned later, I could see that he must have been very stuck; mud and rock had been slung all over. Looks like he had it buried in the hubs at one point.

I also have been known to load dogs and then go to work! This requires certain dogs to be taken—ones that will not bark in the dog box. As a pastor, I do a lot of visits, and I can't have a pack of rabbit-crazed beagles barking in the hospital parking garage. I do pastoral visits—after the person has followed me 45 minutes away to a hospital—and then, after the visits, I sneak off to get a quick hunt in before evening meetings. It is a good system. I am so good at catching people tailing me now that I could be in one of those action blockbusters.

"Don't you think you are a little paranoid?" My wife rolled her eyes.

"Nope," I said, "I know that Dodge behind me. He's a rabbit hunter. Watch what happens when I stop here for coffee." Sure enough, the guy stopped with me, staying at the other end of the convenience store parking lot until I left, and then he resumed the tail.

"How did you know that would happen?" Renee asked.

"When I pull up to a hunting spot and see a truck parked there, I take notice. It happens a lot."

Then, I found the best method yet for getting into my spots. Or at least some of them. I take my wife's little SUV. It can't get to all coverts, but the little thing can get into lots of places. The dog box will not fit in the back hatch, so I just let them run around the back seat and ricochet off the windows. No one expects to see me in that car—they expect that to be Renee. I can sneak past people in town, who never think to follow that car. I remember the first time I did this trick, and I was flabbergasted at the amount of nose prints on the windows, and it looked like enough dog hair stuck to the upholstery to make an entire quilt for a king sized bed. After the hunt, I unloaded the dogs and refrigerated the rabbits, and Renee said, "I have to run out and do errands for my Mom! I will be back."

She was gone for two minutes. The phone rang. It was Renee. "You are in so much trouble, mister," she said.

"Is it the dog hair?"

"What?"

"Oh, I was gonna clean that up off the back seat, but you left too fast."

"Wow," Renee said, "I didn't notice that! UGGH!"

"Is it the nose smudges on all the windows?"

"Is that what that is? That is on the inside? Man, that is a mess."

I basically gave her two things to get angry about that she didn't even know. "Well," I said, "Why am I in trouble?"

"You borrowed my car and returned it with a 1/8 of a tank is all?"

"I learned that from a friend of mine," I said.

Summer Feral

We are nearly at the time of year when driving gets a bit easier since the school buses will be parked for summer recess! COVID, being COVID, really made for a sad winter for our kids because there were no snow days! The pandemic has schools perfectly equipped to teach remotely and the kids just log on from home, regardless of weather. Snow days were one of my favorite things in the whole world when I was a kid. There is no suspense on snow days now. When my stepson was still in high school, the notification had no hint of drama—the school had a robot call each parent at 6:30 in the morning and inform us that school had either been canceled or delayed for two hours due to inclement weather. They also sent a text with the same information. Instant gratification, and half the time, the kids never found out until late morning when they emerged from their slumber.

Way back in my childhood, a snowy morning was full of mystique. First of all, meteorologists, as inaccurate as they can be now, were even more vague then—before supercomputers took over the job. When they did know that snow was coming, no one knew for sure how big it might be. I lived on the outer edge of lake effect snow off Lake Eerie, and we might get a dusting of snow or over a foot, depending on the wind direction and temperature. Snowflakes get smaller as the air temperature gets colder. When it was barely below freezing, the flakes were huge and fluffy. A "warm up" to 30 degrees after weeks of zero temps would have massive flakes falling onto frozen ground, and the snow accumulated fast instead of melting as it landed.

So, we would wake up and turn on the radio. I can't tell you the last time I listened to the radio. Pandora and satellite radio are how I roll these days—Bluegrass channel on the truck's satellite radio, Waylon Jennings on my computer's Pandora. As a kid, the family huddled around the radio and just listened. We listened to it as we ate breakfast every day, but we really tuned in when it snowed. After every couple of songs, the DJ would break in and give a list of closings and two-hour delays. We kids waited with Christmas-like anticipation, waiting for our school to be listed. Then, a resurgence of hope as schools gradually upgraded from a delay to cancellation.

Then, summer arrived, and we had to make up all those school days. A bad winter would gobble up a bunch of days that we should have been off—Good Friday and Easter Monday, among other days—and when those days were exhausted, we would add days at the end, often extending into mid-June. That made for long days at school, staring out the window as the trees were resurgent green and the air was warm. The nicer it got, the shorter our attention spans became. Even so, I loved snow days and would not have wanted to lose them, especially since rabbit season was during the winter!

It seemed like everyone was outside all the time back then, and nowadays, most people view outdoors as something to be briefly endured between vehicles and buildings, living most of the time in front of screens (computers, televisions, and phones) and in central air conditioning and modern heating with a thermostat in almost every room to customize each person's comfort! Last summer, I had to break away from it all. Covid had shut things down. The Governor closed restaurants. People were losing their minds as if cooking was a lost art and no one knew how to do it anymore. To be honest, I am embarrassed at the amount of money I saved in 2020 just by not going out to eat. Restrictions kept mounting, and my job as a pastor was really altered as clergy were not permitted to do hospital or nursing home visits at all. Funeral parlors were open, and there were weeks when I had two or three funerals. They were not Covid funerals but were mostly people without any church membership. Many pastors stopped doing funerals for non-church members during the pandemic. I would never refuse to help a family. So, my weekdays became funerals and talking on the phone. Talking on the phone replaced visits. I have never talked on the phone so much in my whole life. I ordered rechargeable headphones that connected via Bluetooth to my cell phone. For the first time in 25 years of ministry, I was unable to sit with families in the hospital as a loved one was in surgery—the families were not allowed in the hospital either!

Then, I realized something: I could talk on the phone from anywhere. My wife works at the University, and she was relegated to online work from home, too. She was dealing with curriculum issues while I was talking with families and praying with patients. Sometimes we would get in each other's way, her talking in online meetings and me talking very loudly with someone hard of hearing. Not that my hearing is perfect! I call my truck the Beaglemobile for a reason—It is perfectly set up for living with hounds on the road. Dog box in the bed, a tent on top, and a few amenities, including an awning that can be deployed, which gives shade and has a screen house that zips onto it—a perfect place to sit on a rainy day or mosquito-filled evenings.

"I am gonna go run dogs," I said to my wife, Renee, on a Monday. This is not rare for me to say.

"Coming home for supper?" She asked.

"No," I answered.

"I didn't figure," she said, "It isn't dark until late, and I know you usually run dogs until dark. What do you want me to cook? I will have some here when you get home."

"I ain't coming home until Friday," I said.

"What?" She wrinkled her eyebrows in disbelief.

"If my job has been reduced to talking on the phone, I may as well be someplace I like."

"I guess that makes sense," she said.

"I will take all the dogs," I said.

"Good!" Renee's eyes lit up, "When they bark during meetings, I have to mute Zoom and get them quiet."

"I am going to the beagle club," I said.

"Which one?" She asked. I belong to two clubs; both are fenced enclosures where we stock rabbits that are legally box-trapped in the winter and transported. It makes for a higher population of bunnies and is where we hold field competitions.

"West Branch," I said. That club has four separate enclosures, and I wouldn't be as likely to interfere with other club members or monopolize the running grounds.

I filled the cooler with food and ice packs—the ice packs were frozen quart bags of venison, rabbit, and game birds from the last hunting season. I stashed some pasta and other dry goods in my truck, too—stuff packaged in paper or cardboard, packaging that could be used for fire starter at night and would make for easy disposal. I didn't want dirty cans around camp, attracting critters. I have a portable charger made by Goal Zero, and it allows me to charge tracking collars and my cell phone. Off I went!

I soon set up a routine. Put dogs on the ground and let them run rabbits from dawn until about ten o'clock in the morning, working on Sunday's sermon. Then, I would get them water and let them spend the heat of the day in the shade. I would cook a meal for myself at about eleven o'clock in the morning and commence making all the phone calls to hospitalized church members and the shut-ins, whether they be in their own house or a nursing home. As the hot afternoon sun was setting, I would cut dogs loose again, giving them a few more hours of chase. I would feed the dogs and cook another meal before building a campfire. I would put the dogs on tie-out stakes and the pack of beagles, and I would stare into the fire. Canine and humans huddled around the flames, an act as ancient as humanity itself. Some anthropologists believe that it was the domestication of the wolf into dogs almost 30,000 years ago that was what really made humans a successful species—we became much better hunters with the addition of the dog. The dogs became successful, too, as they had human technology and weapons to help—the dog didn't have to catch the animal; we humans could kill from a distance.

At my campsite, dogs would sprawl out on the grass, flames dancing in their eyes until their eyelids closed, and the sounds of gentle snoring added a rhythmic accompaniment to the sparks and pops of the fire. I kept a mountain dulcimer in the truck, and sometimes, I would get it out and pick a few songs. Sometimes, I played for hours. I used the time to practice and get better at playing. I would put the dogs back into the safety of the truck's dog box before climbing into my rooftop tent. No TV, no computer, no refrigeration, no microwave. Well, I had the phone, which is a computer, but I mostly used it as—get this—a phone. We live in a world where texting is more valued than conversation. I check my email once per day and answer texts a couple of times per day.

It would be a mistake to say that my wife is a camping enthusiast, but she isn't opposed to camping either—especially since my rooftop tent has a built-in mattress. My wife spent two nights with me that first week afield, and she brought some fresh ice cubes and food. She enjoyed seeing the dogs and would help me run dos in the evening. Heck, I think if I had internet she may have stayed with me all week. When I got up to run dogs in the morning, she would head back home to go to work online.

I returned on Friday night—I broke camp in the afternoon, ran dogs in the evening, and went home with tired and content dogs. Sunday, after church, I packed the truck again.

"I am going to the beagle club tomorrow," I announced as I put the last batch of gear in the roof rack. I have a zippered bag that attaches there, and I put all my bedding, pillows, and clothing on top. It was light but bulky, and I had everything in huge garbage bags made for contractors. The bags ensured that they would stay dry in the event of rain.

"Oh, mixing it up this week with a different club?"

"Yeah," I said, "And I told the guys I would do some fence work where a deer kicked it down."

"Sounds like fun," Renee rolled her eyes sarcastically.

"It won't be too bad. I can do it while making my pastoral visits by phone or using headphones. Hands-free."

"I will be out on Wednesday!" She said, "I will stop at Hog's Galore and get the marinaded pork chops to cook that night."

"Sounds good to me," I said.

This roaming hound life got to be a regular thing. My wife got really happy when I decided to go camp near a hunting spot that was near a pristine trout stream. "I will bring you home some trout," I said. As the weather warmed, I moved to a spot where I could catch some catfish for Renee. I caught some panfish, too— I am partial to perch. My body adjusted to sleeping when it was dark and being up early to greet the sun. The insomnia that can come from looking at screens all day faded away. I adjusted to a slower pace. I took pleasure in cooking and finding creative ways to do it. Open fire cooking. Propane when the fire risk was high in the driest part of summer.

I would come home and find that the COVID restrictions were expanded—Restaurants were not allowed to serve beer after ten o'clock at night, and no one could sit at the bar or drink any alcohol unless they were eating food. Once they were done eating, they had to quit drinking. People were outraged at this. I was wondering why people felt a need to be sitting at the bar without food on a weeknight at midnight, but I simply said, "Oh, I didn't know about the changes," when someone grumbled to me about it on the phone. I spent Saturdays doing laundry, and on Sundays, I would go grocery shopping. I got good at getting ready to eat food for rainy days when cooking was not going to be easy—mixed nuts, breakfast cereal, and homemade venison jerky. I bought small individual-sized milk containers for cereal and coffee. In August, I picked blackberries for Renee. I found new hunting spots. I didn't go every week, but many. Often to the beagle clubs, where Renee would stay a few nights. She got to enjoy the time away from the screens and noise and news. I didn't mind not being flooded with the news, and my daily log of phone calls allowed me to keep up just fine with current events without having to park in front of cable news.

I once heard Richard Louv speak at a gathering of Outdoor Writers. He has several books in print, one of which is titled "Last Child in the Woods." He coined the phrase "nature deficit disorder," which sounds a bit like attention deficit disorder. He argues that kids do not get outside enough. They don't roam natural places like kids from previous generations. I was thinking about that a lot last summer as people were distraught about not seeing concerts, not sitting at the bar, and having lots of rules for restaurants. I was fishing, camping, running dogs, picking berries and doing anything I wanted.

"The problem," I said to a friend, "Is we are allowed to go outside; we just can't go out."

"What?"

"And going out isn't really going outside. They should call it going in. It is all about going into a bar, or restaurant, or theater, or something. Going outside is where it is at! Much better."

This summer, things are less strict. Bars are open. Restaurants are at almost full capacity. I am allowed to do nursing home visits again, and some hospital visits. Vaccines are present. This summer will be better for people who struggled last year. I had an easy time last summer, just because I like being outside! Hound music every day!

I was recently in the yard when I heard my wife come up behind me and say, "Uh oh."

"What?"

"You are staring at your truck."

"Yeah, I need tires."

"And?"

"And what?"

"You are getting the urge to hit the road and get off of it somewhere with briars!"

"Yeah, I guess so."

"Summer feral."

"What? I stopped staring at my tires and looked at Renee.

"I told people last summer that you had gone feral," she said, "Or partly feral, living outside most of the summer."

"HA!" I laughed, "I won't be gone as much this summer."

"Make sure you are gone for blackberry season," she winked and hugged me tight. Let's go out. Less, and outside more.

www.ingramcontent.com/pod-product-compliance
Lightning Source LLC
Chambersburg PA
CBHW021229090426
42740CB00006B/450